THE USA IN WORLD WAR I

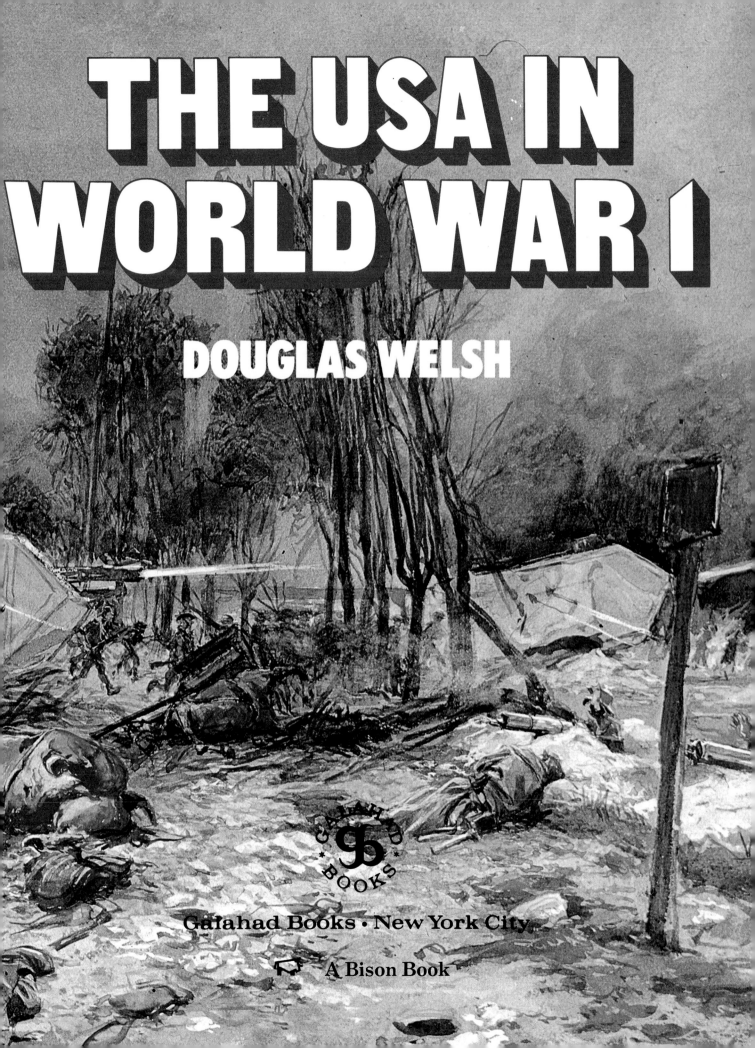

THE USA IN WORLD WAR I

DOUGLAS WELSH

Galahad Books • New York City

A Bison Book

First Published in the US by
Galahad Books
a division of A & W Publishers, Inc.
95 Madison Avenue
New York
New York 10016

Copyright © 1982 Bison Books Limited

Produced by
Bison Books Limited
4 Cromwell Place
London SW7

Library of Congress Catalog Card Number
81-86651

ISBN 0-88365-601-9

Printed in Hong Kong

CONTENTS

1 CLINGING TO NEUTRALITY

World War I was America's 'great adventure' into the affairs of the world powers. It would prove to be a time for discovery of 'self' and a sense of direction, but it would also hold many disappointments that would disillusion the powerful young nation.

After the statement of the Monroe Doctrine in 1823 the United States had concerned itself primarily with its own hemisphere and with the realization of the goals of its 'Manifest Destiny' on the North American continent. It had, for the most part, kept itself aloof from European affairs. In Europe, America was regarded as a second or third rate power in spite of the fact that its brief war with Spain in 1898 clearly indicated America's potential. Yet, in the event, the American nation, although looked upon as an uncouth adolescent by the mature, well-established Europeans, became involved in European affairs when the destiny of the world hinged on its participation in those affairs. America took its role as a world power and in so doing lost the 'innocence' of its youth.

Below: Archduke Franz Ferdinand and his wife arrive in Sarajevo

When the nationalistic fervor of Serbia's pledge to free all Slavs from the control of the Austro-Hungarian Empire erupted with the assassination of Archduke Franz Ferdinand on 28 June 1914 the stage was set for yet another war on the European continent. After a bitter month of confrontation and tension Austria-Hungary declared war on Serbia on 28 July. Germany aligned itself with Austria-Hungary against the Serbians. Russia, a Slavic nation, rose immediately to Serbia's defense. By fall other nations had joined the coalitions being formed. On 1 August Germany declared war on Russia and two days later declared war on France, a long-standing ally of Russia. On 4 and 12 August Britain declared war on Germany and Austria-Hungary respectively.

America however sought to preserve its neutrality. Europe was notorious for its wars which drew some nations to the brink of disaster while other European countries stood at the sidelines. America had more important problems to concern itself with than the squabbles in Europe. As many new Americans pointed out, they had come to America to escape the European war cycles. Peace was revered as a national treasure. True, America had had wars and conflicts of its own, but it was considered one thing to die for a cause at home and quite another to die on foreign soil over the pettiness of empires in Europe.

The desire for neutrality was also fed by the fact that America was the 'Great Melting Pot' of the world. Although language, customs and laws were based on the British system, large segments of the American population were from Eastern and Western Europe and the Mediterranean. Involvement in the war would be difficult for first- or second-generation immigrants. Although the United States urged a new nationalism of its own, whether the country decided to enter the war on the side of Britain and France or Germany and Austria-Hungary, there would be those who would be opposed to fighting against the citizens of their 'old country.'

Thus in 1914 President Woodrow Wilson urged the nation to support neutrality in theory and practice and to be impartial in its assessment of the events in Europe. With their sympathies divided the American people could not remain idle. Some became indirectly involved in the war by participating in fund-raising

Above: President Woodrow Wilson (1865–1924) had been President of Princeton University and Democratic Governor of New York before being elected to the Presidency in 1912. He won the 1916 election on the slogan 'He Kept Us Out of War.' German submarine attacks and the Zimmerman Telegram incident brought America into the war but Wilson still tried to maintain an idealistic attitude to foreign affairs questions. His plans for a postwar League of Nations were never properly achieved.
Right: One of the many posters appealing for recruits for the US services.

organizations such as the German Relief Fund. Others chose more active roles by enlisting as volunteers in the British, Canadian and French Armies. One such group was the Lafayette Escadrille, American aviators who joined the French Air Force (*see* Chapter 4). It was obvious quite early in the war that maintaining a neutral stance would be difficult. Wilson could only hope that the war in Europe would end before this became impossible.

As the months passed Wilson's fears slowly materi-alized. By mid-1915 the war had begun to bog down. On the Eastern Front Germany and Austria-Hungary were overpowering the ponderous, archaic Russian military machine but they could not achieve a de-cisive victory. On the Western Front trenches divided Europe from the English Channel to the border of Switzerland. Neither side had been able to gain an easy victory, but it appeared as though Germany had the upper hand. The Allies had succeeded in scoring quick victories around the world as British naval power helped compel the German colonies to surrender one after another.

The initial effectiveness of the Allies at sea created the situation which would eventually draw the United States into the war. Both the Allies and the Central Powers realized that as the war was prolonged, the ability of any participant to continue would diminish unless a steady flow of supplies could be maintained. Britain controlled the seas, her fleet still second to none. Although Germany attempted to challenge that control there was usually little doubt that the German fleet would fail in surface engagements. Consequently the likelihood of ships, even those flying neutral flags, reaching German ports was slim, while Britain and France continued to enjoy virtually uninterrupted trade. To counter Britain's fleet, Germany chose to utilize the submarine to its fullest potential.

America was about to be caught in the middle of the war on the open sea. It was actually Britain which first provoked a confrontation. As a neutral nation the United States believed it had the right to continue to trade with any country free of threat, as long as international restrictions on supplying contraband to any of the belligerent nations were adhered to. The British refused to recognize America's claims, pointing out that shipments of food could feed enemy armies, raw materials could be used to manufacture arms, and even cloth and buttons might make uniforms. Britain had extended her blockade not only around German ports but around Norway, Sweden and Denmark. Foreign ships approaching the European continent were ordered to British ports, where a system of search and seizure was employed. Goods were confiscated depending on British needs at any given time. The value of goods declared to be contraband by the British was not reimbursed. The United States declared this policy illegal and charged Britain with flagrant violation of the rights of neutrality. The issue became so heated that for a time it appeared there would be a confrontation between Britain and the United States.

International law decreed that ships could be halted and searched. It also required that if a contraband-carrying ship could not be taken to a port its passengers and crew were to be given protection before the ship could be sunk. When Germany entered the naval war with its submarines, adherence to this decree became very difficult. The judgment of the commander of a submarine or orders from superior government officials could be used to justify attacks on vessels believed to be carrying contraband. It was obvious that the German naval situation could make the loss of civilian lives unavoidable.

Although the British tended to disregard the rights of neutral American shipping the introduction of German submarines would prove to be a far more deadly threat. The reaction of President Wilson made

Top: The liner *Lusitania* seen here on a voyage from Liverpool to New York in 1907. When the *Lusitania* was sunk 1153 passengers were killed. This provoked strong anti-German feeling in the United States which, despite the claim that the *Lusitania* was carrying arms, persuaded the German government to restrict the operations of their submarine force.

Above: The body of one of the dead American passengers from the *Lusitania* is brought ashore at Queenstown in Ireland. Pictures like this helped inflame American opinion.
Top right: Captain Turner commanded the *Lusitania* on its last, ill-fated voyage.

it clear that his neutralist policies leaned more heavily in favor of Britain and her allies. When warned by Germany that there was evidence that the United States was trading in contraband with Britain and France, Wilson promptly replied that warfare using submarines was 'totally abhorrent' and that Germany would be 'held accountable' for any loss of American lives or property on the high seas. It was a case of challenge being answered by challenge. Allied propaganda was already being displayed by American newspapers and the submarine issue gave added fuel to the growing antagonism toward the Central Powers.

Germany was therefore faced with a dilemma. It was obvious that a decision on policy had to be made and the various aspects of the issue had to be carefully weighed. The United States was a relatively unknown quantity, whose participation in the war on behalf of the Allies might not really be of great consequence. It would take the United States time to mobilize and train an army and it would be even more difficult to transport that army to Europe. The Central Powers' hopes of winning the war depended largely on maintaining the submarine blockade. It was a delicately balanced strategy of attempting to 'starve' the Allies before the Central Powers met that same fate. Evidence from German agents and sympathizers in the United States indicated that it was only a matter of time before America began openly supporting the Allies, if not actively participating in the war. Thus the German

General Staff decided that it was better to maintain the pressures of the blockade and risk antagonizing the United States than to allow supplies to slip through to the Allies. Any ship discovered sailing in waters which the German Navy was blockading would be considered hostile and would be sunk on sight.

On 28 March 1915, shortly after Wilson's warning, a British steamer was torpedoed off the Irish coast. The vessel sank and many of the American passengers on board were killed. The attack resulted in a public outcry in the United States which was mildly tempered by the fact that the vessel was British. Two months later, on 7 May 1915, 128 Americans lost their lives when the British liner *Lusitania* was sunk off the southern coast of Ireland. Germany claimed that the *Lusitania* was carrying war materials, which in fact she was, and justified its actions by reminding the international community that the German government had published warnings next to any newspaper advertisements for the *Lusitania* explaining their beliefs and attempting to persuade those who might wish to sail on the vessel that their lives could be in danger.

Public outrage was widespread and the *Lusitania* issue could not be quietly allowed to pass. The US State Department's protests over the sinking carried the additional warning that the repetition of such an incident would have serious repercussions. American anger was still unabated when in August the British liner *Arabic* was sunk and two more Americans were killed. It appeared as though the US and Germany were on a collision course. In response to the American outcry the German government issued a statement on 1 September 1915 that in future passenger liners would not be attacked without warning, provided the liners did not attempt to offer resistance or escape. That promise temporarily defused a potentially explosive situation. Most Americans who continued to favor neutrality accepted that the honor of the United States had been upheld and that a victory for the cause of neutrality had been won by the protests and show of firmness.

The cases of the *Lusitania* and the *Arabic* serve to illustrate the delicacy of the situation. The fact that the conflict in Europe could so easily spread to include the US made the maintenance of a neutral position seem impossible. For six months Germany fulfilled its pledge. Then, in March 1916, the French passenger vessel *Sussex* was attacked. In that six-month period the influx of contraband goods to the Allies had increased. President Wilson threatened to break off diplomatic relations with Germany unless submarine warfare was abandoned. Germany replied with the '*Sussex* Pledge,' stating that they would return to their previous stance on attacking passenger vessels if the US intervened to . influence the British blockade polices. According to the German government that blockade had inflicted severe distress and devastating food shortages on the German people, leaving the women and children of Germany ill and hungry. However, the United States would not become involved by assenting to modifications of the original promises, claiming that the blockade issue was strictly between Germany and Britain. The only aspect that concerned America was German violation of US neutrality on the open sea.

At the same time as those issues were reaching a climax, American public opinion became more divided over Wilson's methods of dealing with the Central Powers. Many thought Wilson should be firmer, after the pattern of former President Theodore Roosevelt. Others believed that Wilson's threats had actually gone too far and that he was needlessly involving the US in European matters. Yet others thought that it should be the responsibility of Congress to stop the US from becoming in any way influenced by any of the belligerent nations. Wilson had his own course to follow and in June 1916 the National Defense Act was passed with the aim of strengthening the US armed forces. A three-year naval program was also instituted. The United States Shipping Board was created to oversee an accelerated ship-construction program to meet the country's needs in the event of active participation in the war. The Council of National Defense was also established with responsibility for the mobilization of the nation's resources. Although it appeared that Wilson had given up all hope of remaining neutral, he justified the National Defense Act and the creation of the two commissions as displays of strength necessary to reaffirm American neutrality. Wilson's primary campaign slogan for the 1916 Presidential Election, 'He kept us out of war,' helped win him the election and proved that the American people continued to rely on his course of action and his neutralist policies.

After several more months of relative calm Germany decided to renew unrestricted submarine warfare on 1 February 1917. The German government had again weighed the risks of drawing the US into the war and decided that if the United States declared war on the Central Powers, American aid would be too late in arriving to do any good. Wilson accepted the abolition of the restrictions as a direct challenge to the United States and broke off diplomatic relations with Germany on 3 February. Although at the brink of war, America still clung to peace. It was the Allies, recognizing their need for American involvement and aid, who tipped the balance. On 24 February 1917 British Intelligence passed an intercepted German message to the American Ambassador in Britain. The message, from the German Foreign Secretary to the German Minister in Mexico, became known as the 'Zimmerman Telegram.'

The message applied for Mexican support in the event of the US entering the war. Mexico was asked to attack the United States to recapture areas, including New Mexico, Arizona, and Texas, which had previously been Mexican. On 1 March 1917 President Wilson released copies of the Zimmerman Telegram to the Associated Press. America was shocked and angered and there was little doubt what the response of the nation would be. On 12 March it was announced that all merchant vessels operating in the war zones would be armed and had permission to defend themselves if the need arose. Eight days later Wilson called an emergency meeting of his Cabinet to discuss long-standing grievances against Germany. He then called for a special joint session of Congress to be held on 2 April 1917.

On that date President Wilson delivered his 'War Message.' Standing before Congress Wilson condemned German submarine warfare and the loss of American lives, outlined the challenge to humanity, and described the need to right the wrongs being perpetrated by Germany. Wilson's idealistic rhetoric gave the United States the chance to enter the war with a clear conscience, knowing that the nation was taking this step not for private gain but to make the world safe for democracy once again. Wilson firmly believed that the nation would be willing to sacrifice anything to accomplish that end. War was declared and on 4 and 6 April respectively the United States Senate and House of Representatives ratified the declaration. America was committed to the war and the 'great adventure' had begun.

2 MOBILIZATION FOR WAR

The war had finally come to America. The idealistic dreams of neutrality and peace were shattered. Although the nation moved to a wartime spirit and young men rushed to join the armed services in answer to the call, America was essentially physically unprepared to support its verbal declaration. Neither the embellished rhetoric of that declaration nor the will to fight for the established cause provided an ability to exercise military influence.

JOIN THE ARMY AIR SERVICE BE AN AMERICAN EAGLE!
CONSULT YOUR LOCAL DRAFT BOARD, READ THE ILLUSTRATED BOOKLET AT ANY RECRUITING OFFICE, OR WRITE TO THE CHIEF SIGNAL OFFICER OF THE ARMY, WASHINGTON, D.C.

WAKE UP, AMERICA!

CIVILIZATION CALLS EVERY MAN WOMAN AND CHILD!
MAYOR'S COMMITTEE 50 EAST 42ⁿᵈ ST

Initially the United States did not appear to recognize the scope of mobilizing, training, supplying and transporting men, arms and equipment across the Atlantic to France, when only there could American involvement have any impact. The United States had a standing army but the number of troops in that army was only a minute fraction of the force needed to fight the type of war being waged in Europe. American troop training procedures and tactics were a far cry from the demands imposed by European

Above & above left: Recruiting posters used easily recognizable symbols like the Stars and Stripes and the American eagle and many also emphasized the total effort which would be required.

Left: The first numbers are drawn after the passing of the Selective Service Act in 1917.
Bottom: The movie actress Theda Bara makes a speech during the 4th Liberty Loan Drive.
Bottom right: Women workers in an armaments factory. As in many other countries the demands of war brought women into many occupations that had previously been regarded as male preserves.
Below: Draftees from New York on the way to their training camp in the summer of 1917.

trench warfare. Only the US Navy had a viable role which it could immediately play in the war, and it would grow more capable through its participation in antisubmarine and escort duty as the months continued. In essence, America was 'ready to fight but not fighting ready.'

This fact, though not fully appreciated by the United States, did not escape the German High Command. Germany, which had long recognized American sympathy for the Allies' position, had calculated the length of time it would take the US to achieve a stable war footing. Their minimum estimates were six to eight months, with a more likely schedule of at least 12 months, before America could put its full resources behind the war effort. That estimate gave the German High Command a period of security during which to exercise unrestricted submarine warfare and launch a determined campaign in France to turn the tide irreversibly against the Allies. The German government realized that once these options had been played, if their efforts failed, American involvement would mean defeat for the Central Powers.

America's immediate task was the mobilization of its full resources. Manpower was of primary importance. The American military realized that the style and scope of the war in Europe would require hundreds of thousands of men, far more than would be raised by the initial fervor of volunteers in the emotional aftermath of the declaration of war. On 18 May 1917 Congress ratified the Selective Service Act, requiring all American males between the ages of 21 and 30 to register for active duty. By August 1918 it had become evident that this age bracket could not provide the numbers of men that modern warfare demanded and on 31 August the Selective Service Act was amended to include men between the ages of 18 and 45.

The initial Selective Service measure brought more than 24,000,000 men under registration. Of the

4,500,000 who eventually served their country during the war, 3,000,000 were inducted into the army. By late summer and fall of 1917 2,000,000 men had joined the military as a result of voluntary enlistment or through the Selective Service Act. Those numbers quickly made it obvious that the available US training facilities were inadequate for the influx of men. Established camps became 'tent cities' overnight. Billets normally used to quarter troops were converted into officers' quarters and administration centers. Many new camps were established, primarily on the east coast where troops would have easy access to ports of embarkation.

For the first time since the American Civil War all racial groups within American society were drawn into the military. Of the more than 370,000 black Americans who served, 200,000 were sent to Europe. However, the racial situation in the United States was reflected in the armed forces and most racial minorities, particularly blacks and American Indians, were segregated and employed in primarily noncombat roles. It was erroneously believed that black soldiers lacked the courage to fight and military leaders assigned them to administration, supply and the medical corps. However, several all-black regiments, such as the 369th Infantry Regiment, saw combat and their abilities and courage were unquestionable.

There were, however, more pressing issues than merely taking men from civilian life and attempting to train them. Financing the war effort was of primary concern. The war would cost tens of billions of dollars and Congress had to devise methods for securing those funds. It was decided that 66 percent of all money needed would be 'borrowed' by the government. Victory Loan and Liberty Loan drives were instituted through which War Bonds were sold. The government applied every possible means to encourage sales of War Bonds. Posters proclaimed the patriotism of those who bought bonds. Clubs and civic groups of all types displayed their support by hosting purchasing drives. Even new-found heroes and heroines of the infant movie industry like Douglas Fairbanks, Charlie Chaplin and Mary Pickford made public appearances to urge the masses to invest in their nation through War Bonds. More than $21 billion was eventually raised through bond sales. The other 33 percent of funds needed was destined to be raised through taxation. Taxes were imposed on income. Alcohol, tobacco, telephone and telegraph messages, railroad tickets and even certain forms of public amusement became liable to federal taxation.

The mobilization of American industries was next to be considered. The War Industries Board was established in 1917 and soon dominated all manufacturing in the United States. Not only did the Board establish the criteria of war production, but also helped establish new industries to meet the war demands. The production of nonessential goods was carefully monitored and waste in industries was virtually eliminated. Before the war ended the War Industries Board regulated the production of more than 30,000 different items.

Congress also gave the President sweeping wartime powers. This permitted the President to set prices, to regulate and even take national possession of industries such as mining, food processing, transport and communication. The majority of these presidential powers were maintained through commissionary boards such as the War Industries Board. The War Finance Corporation controlled the lending of public funds to businesses which were converting to war production. The Emergency Fleet Corporation was, by the end of the war, actually producing ships more rapidly than the Germans could hope to sink them. The Railroad Administration controlled, operated and set rates and wages for all railroads, keeping them efficient for best possible service to the war effort. The Fuel Administration monitored the use of national resources such as coal and oil and encouraged their efficient use by industry and the public.

Along with industry, labor was required to do its share. Almost one year after war was declared Wilson established the National War Labor Board and several

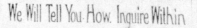

Beat back the HUN with LIBERTY BONDS

months later the War Labor Policies Board. These agencies were intended to keep labor and management on a course most advantageous to the nation and the war. They had the power to arbitrate disputes and set policy for wages, working hours and conditions.

The Federal Food Administration was created to regulate quantities and prices of food, assuring adequate supplies for both military and civilian needs. The administration was also successfully involved in agricultural relief programs to the Allies. 'Victory Gardens' and the observance of 'wheatless' and 'meatless' days were encouraged. Every effort was made to curb the anxieties of the people over possible shortages of food and make the public conscious of the disastrous effects of hoarding and waste.

Public opinion was an intangible commodity which had also to be mobilized and monitored. The Committee on Public Information was formed. Leaflets and posters were distributed and speechmakers, known for their famous 'four minute' rallying orations, travelled around the country to sell the war to

Left: Propaganda posters commonly emphasized German 'brutality.'
Far left top: Marine units served with the Army in France.
Far left bottom: Campaigns were waged against wasting food.
Below: British fishermen welcome an American destroyer force.

the American people and promote the nationalistic emotions of the masses. The populace was indeed mobilized. From schools and churches to fraternal organizations and women's groups the 'duty of every red-blooded American' was proclaimed. The Committee on Public Information was at its roots a propaganda organization with responsibility for releasing information on American aims and the goals of her allies, while denouncing the actions of the German government and Central Powers. In industry, labor, agriculture and in homes across America, the nation was geared for victory.

America was reaching its full mobilization on the 'Home Front' and had now to concern itself with active involvement in the war in Europe and at sea. The navy, as stated, was the only effective fighting force during those early days. It had not turned a blind eye to the inevitability of the war. American seamen knew all too well the scope of the German threat on the seas and when war was officially declared American naval personnel had a relatively clear understanding of the role they would play. First, if the United States was to aid its allies, large concentrations of troops, supplies and materiel would have to be transported across what was considered the most dangerous stretch of water in the world. The North Atlantic was infamous for its storm fury. However, the worst threat was the German U-Boat. It was useless to work on the various aspects of military readiness if the European Continent could not be reached. America recognized what Britain and France had come to learn, that to send lone vessels across the open seas was suicidal. Thus the con-

voy system was adopted. Transport vessels were grouped into fleets which were then escorted by warships capable of dealing with enemy vessels. The presence of large numbers of ships and their escorts had several effects. Warships forced U-Boat commanders to be much more cautious. It also meant that in the event of an attack ready assistance would be available to the crew and passengers of damaged or destroyed vessels. The ships usually assigned to convoy duty were destroyers or smaller vessels as maneuverability was the prime requisite.

The US Navy proved so proficient that of the more than 2,500,000 men transported to Europe only a few hundred lives were lost en route. It was an exemplary record and a severely demoralizing blow to the German High Command, who firmly believed that their submarines could nullify the American effort to transfer men and supplies to Europe.

The US Navy operating in European waters was commanded by Admiral William Sims and by the end of the war had established 45 naval bases as far north as Murmansk, Russia, and as far south as Greece. It also aided Britain and France in the endless task of mine laying and sweeping. Although convoy duty, antisubmarine actions and mining operations did not receive the same degree of publicity as some other aspects of the war, without the efficiency of the naval forces the Allied war effort would have been seriously impaired.

In spite of the diligent efforts made by the navy to supply the troops in Europe, the United States had a great deal to learn and overcome. It cost the nation more than $750,000,000 just to feed the army in

Europe, yet the foodstuffs transported were not of the highest quality and rarely reached front-line troops in sufficient quantity. American soldiers were forced to scavenge food, primarily from the French, and 'borrow' shoes and clothing from British and French units when US supply lines broke down. In many of the crucial areas, such as weapons, supplies and even troop training, America appeared clumsy and inept. But the United States would prove surprisingly astute at learning lessons for the future from its European allies.

Although it appeared that America had a long way to go to fulfill its role in the war, positive action was being taken and American troops, though initially few in number, were arriving on the scene. President Wilson placed General John J Pershing in charge of the American Expeditionary Force (AEF) destined for France. 'Black Jack' Pershing was definitely the right man for the job. He not only had a flair for his military duties, but also the political aptitude and awareness necessary for his important position. He had displayed his capabilities in the Spanish American War and in the pacification of the Moros in the Philippines. By 1916 he had returned to the United States to command the forces pursuing the Mexican bandit Pancho Villa.

As commander of the AEF Pershing had a wide understanding of the situation and a deep concern for the average soldier of his command. He had closely followed the development of events in Europe but on reaching France he was appalled by the nonchalance with which British and French commanders accepted their casualty rates. Pershing was not prepared to allow the same fate to befall his own men at the whims of foreign generals whom he judged to be incompetent strategists. With the arrival of the first wave of the AEF the French and British commanders eagerly looked to the Americans as the fresh, vital troops needed to be sent 'over the top.' Pershing immediately crushed such plans by refusing to relinquish control of any American unit or permit troops to enter battle unless the Allies conceded his right to unopposed command of his army in the field. Regardless of the political repercussions, Pershing was not prepared simply to hand his forces to foreign generals who, in his view, had demonstrated a callous disregard for the lives of their troops.

By 4 July 1917 units of the American 1st Infantry Division had landed in France and on that day the 16th Infantry Regiment paraded proudly through the streets of Paris to cheers of 'Vive les Teddies.' The descriptive term 'Yanks' had not yet become the popular manner for referring to American troops. During the ceremonies that day Pershing was given credit for stating, 'Lafayette, we are here,' when he reached Lafayette's tomb. In fact, those immortalized words were spoken by a quartermaster officer, C E Stanton, but the press obviously believed that they

carried more impact if quoted from the general himself.

Once established in France Pershing began to organize a staging area for the American army. The region of Toul-Dijon-Troyes was selected. Its rail lines were not burdened by the French Army and the ports of Saint Nazaire and Marseilles were chosen to handle the 25 tons of cargo scheduled to be landed daily to support the American troops who would be arriving. The 1st Division had moved into the area by 28 July and Pershing was finding it no small task to billet his men adequately. Where possible he housed troops with French villagers and farmers, but the vast majority were forced simply to pitch their tents in the pastures that surrounded the training camp. Efforts were made to keep fraternization with the local population at a minimum and strict regulations, including the curtailment of off-camp liberties, were enacted. The 'innocent' theft of edibles from farms and orchards, even the simple plucking of a handful of berries, were court-martial offenses. Although harsh, these measures were taken in the best interest of the men and the relationship between France and America. The multiplication of one apple or berry taken by the tens of thousands of men who would pass through the camp would have serious repercussions on the local community. Pershing was also well aware that enforcing strict regulations on minor issues would breed the discipline necessary when life and death were at stake.

By 1 September Pershing's Headquarters had been established at Chaumont. Although the location of that command center was common knowledge to the troops and local villagers, news articles referring to Pershing's headquarters began with the mysterious 'Somewhere in France.' At his headquarters Pershing and his staff were wrestling with two primary con-

cerns, men and arms. According to their studies, Pershing announced, nearly 3,000,000 men would be required to defeat the enemy. Such a figure, though relatively accurate, amazed sectors of the American government and the US War Department chose to regard Pershing's assessment as an exaggeration, approaching the manpower question and Selective Service implementation with a much more cautious attitude. They would soon be made to realize their error. Small arms and artillery of all types were needed immediately. There was a great deal of disagreement on precisely what types of weapons should be used. Pershing and his staff indicated that there was a great need for a 105mm howitzer in the artillery branch. However, studies in the States on the development of such a weapon suggested that it would take from two to three years to perfect, by which time the experts concluded the war would be over. The American army was forced to use the available French 75mm light field pieces to meet its needs. In the small arms classification America had two expert manufacturers in the Colt and Browning Companies but in spite of their efforts the need was simply too great and again America was forced to rely on its allies' stockpiles.

In its eagerness to update the American armed forces and keep pace with the new forms of technology, the government, or more precisely the War Department, appropriated millions of dollars for projects which could not possibly meet the deadlines set for their completion. The tank best illustrates this. The army ordered 4400 of two tank models, one light and one heavy, and appropriated $200,000,000 to the program. By the end of the war only 15 American-built tanks had reached Europe, with the bulk of the order still tied up in testing or not even on the production lines. Of the many programs begun only one had any large degree of success. That was the introduction of homing pigeons to the Signal Corps. Of the 25,000 pigeons brought into the program, approximately 15,000 were actually used in France. The remaining 10,000 never left the US. Although the pigeons proved to be extremely reliable and intelligent (95 percent of all messages carried by pigeons were delivered) it was discovered that competent pigeon handlers were much more difficult to train than their feathered messengers.

By October the American 2nd, 26th 'Yankee' and 42nd 'Rainbow' Divisions had arrived. Their average strength was 28,000 men each. Pershing recognized

Left: American infantry and medical personnel during a gas warfare exercise. Troops near the front line had to have gas masks at hand at all times because of the danger from gas shells.
Right: French and American soldiers join in a toast in this picture taken in April 1918.

immediately that their organization was not at all appropriate for the style of warfare being waged. Each division had four infantry regiments, one brigade of artillery and one engineering regiment. It was the multitude of attached support units which were unsuitable and these were either eliminated or strengthened to meet the demands.

As the strength of the AEF grew to more than 100,000 men, the British and French increased pressure on Pershing to commit his troops, trained or untrained, to the front to bolster the thinning Allied lines. Pershing could not be swayed. His troops had received Stateside training but it gave little preparation for the real situation in Europe. He estimated that it would take no less than three months of intensive training before his troops would be ready for assignment to a quiet sector of the front and their 'baptism' in the actual fighting of this peculiar war.

Instructors for the 1st Infantry Division had been chosen from the French 47th Chasseurs Alpins Division, known as the 'Blue Devils.' The French troops were stupified by the lack of adequate training evident in the American ranks. Yet in time the French instructors were also amazed at the speed and dedication with which those same soldiers applied their new training. The use of grenades, trench raiding and gas warfare disciplines were intensively drilled. The extensive training served another purpose. It kept the men's minds from the irregular arrival of supplies, mail and pay caused by the initial disorganization of support groups.

When the three new divisions had arrived Pershing was convinced that the 1st Division was ready for initiation at the front, but he was not prepared to commit the entire division. Pershing and General Pétain of the French High Command agreed on a rotation system whereby one battalion of each regiment in the 1st Division would be assigned to the front for a 10-day period. The Toul sector, approxi-mately 15 miles northeast of Lorraine, was chosen as the location for American reinforcement. For three years that sector had been relatively quiet. Pershing believed that at Toul his green troops could gain confidence without the risk of being caught in a major offensive and being badly mauled or beaten. He did not want to shatter the morale of his virgin army.

On 23 October 1917 the guns of the American 6th Field Artillery Brigade fired America's first shots and America had at last actively joined the ground war in Europe. After 10 uneventful days, punctuated by occasional artillery fire, the initial battalions were replaced. As Pershing inspected the returning troops he could clearly see that their time on the line had been well spent and he was eager to continue this strategy. However, in the previous week the German command had realized that green American troops were now in the line. A warm reception for the American replacements was planned with the intention of humiliating the newly arrived troops and creating a breakdown in American morale.

At midnight on 2 November German forces executed a well-planned raid on the American battalions. Under cover of an artillery barrage German troops cut through the wire and slipped into the trenches, taking 11 prisoners and killing three American soldiers. The inexperienced American troops had taken cover during the assault and it was not until the Germans had accomplished their task that the Americans reacted, killing three German troops.

The incident produced the opposite effect to that which the Germans had intended. Three American lives had now been lost in the trenches of France. The men who were the first to die became heroes and instead of breaking morale the attack gave American troops a cause to rally around. German aggression was no longer a threat merely to the Allies. The loss of American lives had given it a personal significance and the American troops were eager to retaliate.

3 VIRGIN SOLDIERS TO VETERAN ARMY

By November 1917 the four American divisions had completed most of their training and were establishing their winter quarters. Not until February 1918 would the divisions take an active role at the front. However, during the late winter and early spring months both the 26th and 42nd Divisions were involved in confrontations with the enemy that illustrated both the absurdity and horror of warfare in the trenches.

On one occasion the men of the Yankee Division were the target of a trench raid. The night before the raid several large cans of doughnuts had been brought forward as a treat for the men. A seven-man raiding mission struck the units who possessed the doughnuts. When the confrontation ended the American reports stated proudly that no American had perished and while one would-be doughnut snatcher had been killed, not a single pastry had fallen into enemy hands. The 42nd 'Rainbow' Division was the first American unit to experience a gas attack. The 'unnatural weapon' shocked the American troops. It was not only the men at whom the attack was directed who suffered but their rescuers as well. The gas was thought to have dissipated, but lingered in the trenches.

Medical records document cases of men, blinded by the gas, being led to safety by a soldier who through prolonged exposure in the supposedly safe trenches would be blind himself by the time he reached an aid station. It was quickly discovered that once a man had been exposed to the gas the damage was irreparable and no purpose could be served by rushing to his aid. Troops were forced to stand helplessly by while others suffered, leaving the victims behind for rescue much later. Although deadly gases were used throughout the war by both the Allies and the Central Powers, line troops despised the weapon. Its unpredictable nature, especially if the wind shifted, made it as potentially dangerous to the user as to the target.

As spring arrived the Allied Command anticipated massive enemy offensives but where and when were major questions. On 17 April 1918 the American 1st Division was ordered to Cantigny. French troops had been holding the area but the Americans were to take responsibility for it. No sooner had they arrived than German artillery began to bombard the sector. During the average day more than 3500 shells fell along a line which was only 5000 yards long. It was virtually impossible to determine where the trenches had been and the men spent the time between shellings attempting to improve their defenses. Those attempts were generally nothing more than pushing dirt out of shell craters or digging ditches to connect the larger craters so that communication between units could be maintained. The men received one hot meal each night as it was too dangerous to supply rations during the daylight hours.

The 26th Division arrived two days after the 1st and was positioned at the quieter southern end of the line. On 20 April two companies of the 102nd Infantry Regiment moved forward to the village of Seicheprey to relieve the units that had been holding that sector. Their arrival was greeted by a German offensive against the village. By dawn of the following day the battlefield was strewn with American and German dead and the remaining Americans in the village could not hold out against the overwhelming numbers facing them. Both companies were eliminated almost to a man. The few who escaped death or capture gave reports of American troops fighting hand to hand with entrenching tools and of soldiers throwing rocks at the enemy when their ammunition supply was exhausted.

It was America's first actual fight and although the battle was lost the troops gave a good account of themselves. However, the German command realized the immediate advantage of the incident and directed their propaganda services to exploit the encounter.

Above: A machine-gun emplacement by Henry Dunn.
Above right: A wounded Marine is given first aid before being taken to the rear, 22 March 1918. Even in 'quiet' periods trench warfare produced a steady drain of casualties.
Left: American gunners operate a 155mm gun from a well camouflaged position.

They paraded American prisoners behind their lines and broadcast the details of a major American defeat. They attempted to weaken Allied morale by claiming that the Americans could not and would not fight, warning the Allies that if they were depending on the Americans to save them they had been sadly deceived and were no better off than if the Americans had never come. Although the propaganda did for a time bolster German morale in sectors where they opposed American units, it infuriated the American troops and their commanders. More than anything else the American troops and staff wanted a chance to get even with the Germans and prove that they were indeed willing and able to fight.

The Allied command reviewed the front and chose Cantigny village as the target for an American assault. It was considered a good location for American troops to bloody the enemy without great danger of anything going wrong for the Americans. The 28th Infantry Regiment of the 1st Division was chosen to initiate the assault. The men were regular soldiers and although not yet combat veterans they were considered the fighting stock of the US Army. No chances of failure in their endeavor were being taken. A machine-gun battalion, a French flame-thrower detachment and a unit of French tanks were brought forward to assist. Artillery units with 200,000 rounds of ammunition were also positioned to assault the German defenses prior to the infantry attack. Pershing's actual plans were kept so secret that only four line officers knew the details of the operation and the American troops anticipated the arrival of French or British forces for the execution of the advance.

During the night of 27 May the plan for the operation was revealed and the French tanks came into line with the American infantry. At 0545 hours on 28 May the assault began as the 400 guns bombarded the one and one-half mile front. One hour later the bombardment ceased and three waves of American troops went over the top. The artillery barrage had been so devastating that German resistance was virtually non-existent. The troops walked for more than one mile with time to joke and laugh at how easily they were 'putting the Kaiser to rout.' Once inside the village French flame throwers swept away pockets of resistance and more than 250 prisoners were taken. Not only did the assault have the full cooperation of the Allied command but its success was aided by the fact that the Germans had been in the process of rotating troops in that sector and were caught completely unprepared.

Once in the village the 28th Regiment prepared for German counterattacks. Five were launched but only one made a dent in the American lines. At one point the German troops did discover a weak point on the front, but Colonel Theodore Roosevelt Jr rushed his 26th Infantry Battalion forward, closing the gap and repulsing the attack. The village of Cantigny had been captured with approximately 1800 casualties including 199 killed, and this success became a propaganda source for the Allies. Although most of the American commanders realized how heavily weighted the assault had been, an American victory could not have come at a better time.

On the same day that the Americans prepared for their attack at Cantigny a major German offensive broke through the central sector of the front on a course for the Marne and Paris. By early June the German advance had captured some 60,000 French troops and the American forces were about to become completely immersed in the war.

General Ferdinand Foch, Supreme Allied Commander in France, had several experienced French divisions in reserve for just such a German offensive. However, the years of war had taught him that while the enemy attack was at full momentum it was better to send the less experienced troops into the fray first. The enemy would waste men and materiel on such troops and then the veterans could be brought forward to stabilize the front. For this tactic inexperienced troops were needed and the American 2nd and 3rd Divisions fitted that description. Pershing was not at all pleased with the use of his divisions, but in the emergency his hands were tied.

The 2nd Division had seen limited combat but the 3rd was as yet untried. Still they were ordered to the point of the German advance. The 3rd Division was hurried to the front where they joined a French African Colonial unit. Their orders were to hold at the Marne River and to prevent the Germans on the northern bank from crossing the river. The men of the American 7th Machine Gun Battalion and the Colonial forces repulsed two German attempts to cross the only two bridges in their sector. After the second assault it was belatedly decided that the best defense would be the destruction of the bridges. That done the southern bank of the Marne was at least temporarily secured while the remainder of the 3rd Division arrived.

The four regiments of the 2nd Division moved forward on 30 May. The 9th and 23rd Infantry Regiments were regular units with regimental histories dating back to the War of 1812. The 5th and 6th Marine Regiments attached to the division were new

Above: Trucks of the motor transport service are loaded with men of the 7th Infantry who are being taken to a rest area near Moulins.
Left: American infantry and French Schneider tanks during the attack on Cantigny which was the first significant American operation. The Schneider tanks were armed with one 75mm gun and two machine guns. They came into service early in 1917.

and had been added to give the Marines an opportunity to become involved in the war. Their move to the front was one of chaos and confusion. Supply and troop vehicles, as well as fleeing civilians, clogged the roads. The French Tonkinese drivers assigned to transport the 2nd Division had been on the road for more than 72 hours. Through sheer exhaustion several of those drivers fell asleep at the wheel, overturning their vehicles and killing or injuring their American passengers. The American officers were amazed at the situation and asked openly whose side the drivers were on. After two days of struggling to move the division forward on the congested roads the divisional commanders unloaded their men and marched them to the front. As they marched the men sang and joked among themselves about how quickly they would put the Hun to flight. When they arrived at the front this frivolous attitude made the French commanders question their ability to apply themselves to the task at hand. These comments infuriated Colonel Preston Brown, Divisional Chief of Staff, who immediately replied that the men of the 2nd Division were US Army regulars of units which had never lost a battle nor shirked a duty in 100 years of service to their country.

The French troops did not have long to wait to judge for themselves the worth of the American soldiers. On 2 June the German forces continued their advance in the vicinity of the village of Belleau. The 5th Marine Regiment was the target of three determined German assaults but they held their ground. The Marines' obvious fighting spirit and ability took the French commanders by surprise and convinced them that the Americans were capable of making a counteroffensive. The 5th Marines were ordered to move forward and capture the high ground known as Hill 165. By capturing that area a bulge would be formed in the line, thereby partially surrounding the heavily fortified German positions at Belleau Wood. The maneuver was completed and on the afternoon of 6 June the 4th Marine Brigade of the 5th Regiment was given orders to attack Belleau Wood. The 6th Marine Regiment was also moved into the area.

Belleau Wood was no normal forest tract. It covered an area of slightly more than one square mile with growth so thick that it was virtually impossible to see more than five yards in any direction within the forest. The hills and ravines of the wood were perfect defensive terrain. The 4th Brigade did not receive their orders to prepare for an offensive until 1630 hours on 6 June. The assault directives came as a surprise, the officers having told their men to prepare defenses outside the wood in anticipation of a German attack. After 30 minutes of unproductive Allied artillery fire the men were ordered to advance. Almost 500 yards of open wheatfields separated the Marines from the wood, making them easy targets for the German guns. Casualties mounted but the Marines continued

to advance, attempting to isolate and destroy the German positions in an orderly sequence. This proved virtually impossible as the German machine guns had been dispersed to give maximum cross-fire capability. Each time the Americans attempted to outflank one position they were caught by the fire from another. By 2030 hours the Marine units were down to half or even quarter strength. One unit of the 6th Regiment had only 20 men remaining after its efforts to take the village of Bouresches.

For the next 48 hours the 5th Marines continued to eliminate the machine-gun positions in the wood. Supplies and ammunition were desperately low and valiant efforts were made to send aid to the Marines. An ambulance was even used to carry supplies until it was damaged beyond repair by German fire. By 9 June it was obvious that the casualty rate and fatigue of the men made it impossible to continue the assault. The Marines were ordered to withdraw from Belleau Wood and Allied artillery began a six-hour

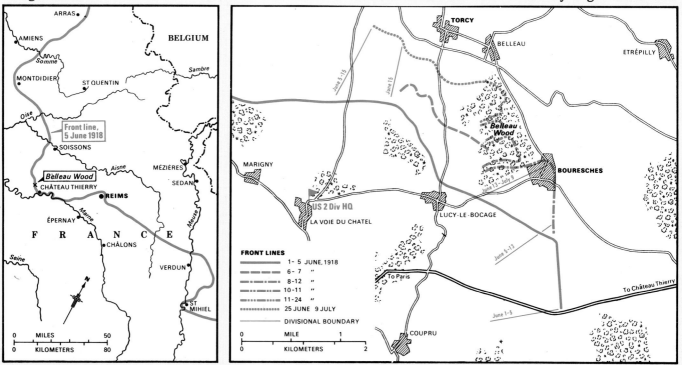

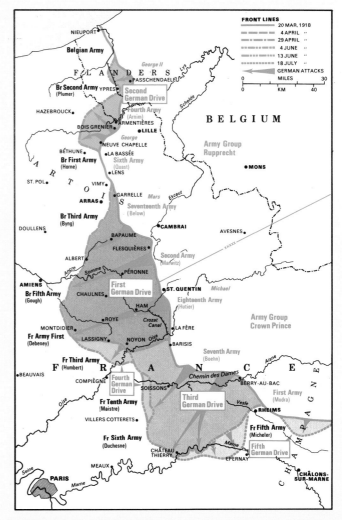

Above: A painting by George Harding showing refugees passing troops going to the front on the Château-Thierry road. The American artillery unit is depicted with French 75mm guns.
Right: The German offensives in the first half of 1918.
Above left: King George V presents Private Harry Shelly with the Medal of Honor. Shelly served with the 33rd Division in the action near Hamel on 4 July.
Below left: The general situation and details of the Belleau Wood action.

barrage of the area. On this occasion their aim was much more accurate and orders were therefore produced for yet another Marine assault. However, the condition of the American units made such a plan impractical.

After three days of rest another assault was launched, preceded by yet another artillery barrage. The advance began and the Marines succeeded in traversing the forest and reaching the northern edge of the wood. On 15 June units of the American 3rd Division joined in the battle to dispose of the last German strongholds in the northwest corner of Belleau Wood. On 25 June after a 14-hour artillery barrage the wood was taken. The battle had raged for 19 days and had cost the Marine regiments dearly. The overall casualty rate was 42 percent, but in individual units it was as high as 95 percent. The Marines had been the focus of attention, not only in Europe but in the States as well. The battle was described in glorifying detail and enlistments in the Marine Corps doubled. An important Marine tradition had been set and the US Army as a whole was credited as being a stubborn, aggressive fighting force.

The 9th and 23rd Regiments of the 2nd Division had waited on the Marines' right flank for the battle

at Belleau Wood to end. Before them lay their objective, the town of Vaux. It was well known that the village had been converted into a veritable fortress. Large casualty rates in assaulting Vaux were expected until the divisional Intelligence Section discovered some valuable information. Through details supplied by a local stonemason, who was familiar with every home in the village, the exact layout of the town was worked out. Aerial and local ground photographs were also used. The assault began near dawn on 1 July. The artillery barrage moved steadily forward at a rate of 100 yards every two minutes. The American infantry regiments followed in the wake of the artillery. Although the German troops fought with their usual doggedness the information the Allies had received proved decisive. The village was taken within half an hour of the infantry advance with a loss of only 46 American lives.

While these attacks were being made the Illinois National Guard Division, designated the 33rd Division, arrived in France. The efforts of the British in supplying weapons for the American forces had exceeded expectations and though not yet fully trained the Illinois Division was fully armed. When the German offensive was renewed the division was

Above: Hindenburg (left) and Ludendorff, the German leaders.
Left: Soldiers of the 32nd Division fire rifle grenades from an unusually well-maintained trench in the Alsace sector.

rushed to the front and ordered to join Australian units in capturing the town of Hamel and surrounding woodlands. The 33rd Division received a great deal of public attention, not only for the importance of its actions but because of the fact that the division was the first front-line unit made up of troops who were neither regular army nor Marines. On 4 July 1918 they began their attack. In one incident a Corporal Thomas Pope single-handedly destroyed a German machine-gun position, holding off enemy attacks until help could arrive. For his efforts he was awarded the Congressional Medal of Honor. It took the division approximately one hour to secure the village and it successfully repulsed a German counterattack the following day. The Australian troops, well known for their fighting ability, paid the highest compliments to the 33rd Division. American troops were indeed proving to be competent, formidable allies.

Throughout the offensive Pershing had become increasingly displeased with the course of events. Although American troops were fighting together as units he wanted an American Army under one command, fighting the battles he wished to fight and not being thrown piecemeal into the lines to reinforce French or British positions or to serve as cannon fodder. Twenty-six American divisions were in France. Seven were at the Front, 15 were training in relatively quiet sectors, two were in reserve and two more were just arriving. Pershing had continued to insist on choosing when American divisions entered the war but he wanted supreme command of how and where they went as well. It was obvious that the Ger-

man armies would attempt one more great offensive, after which the Allies would be ready to attack. Pershing wanted the American divisions together as one army when that time came and set out to achieve that end.

After approximately two weeks of reconsolidation the German offensive began at midnight on 14 July. The location of the drive at Château Thierry had been anticipated as it was the point of deepest German penetration into Allied territory. It was also only 50 miles from Paris. The major physical obstacle to the advance was the Marne River. Once across the river the German command expected to make unimpeded progress to the French capital. Directly in the path of the German advance were four American divisions. At Belleau Wood the 26th Yankee Division had replaced the battle weary 2nd Division. On its right was a French division then the American 3rd Division at Château Thierry, whose machine-gunners had held the bridges six weeks earlier. On the 3rd's right flank was yet another French division and finally the 28th Pennsylvania National Guard Division. The 28th had never been near the line and had been sent to cooperate with the French units in the hope that it would strengthen the Pennsylvanians and maintain their confidence. Their sector was also considered the least likely to receive the main thrust of a German assault. This belief would later result in near disaster. On line away from the other divisions to the east was the veteran 42nd Rainbow Division.

Although the Americans were becoming well known for their defensive abilities the German advance would tax that strength to the limit. On the night of 14 July and throughout the next day the 38th Regiment of the 3rd Division held a position west of where the Surmelin River flowed into the Marne. Links to the main highway to Paris ran through this region and were the German armies' main objectives. The 38th Regiment clung to its positions in efforts to keep the German forces from crossing the river. After being hit with artillery and gas the 38th was forced into hand-to-hand combat as the German troops made their crossing. At 0500 hours the French units began to fall back, as was their custom in the face of such an overwhelming advance. The 30th Regiment of the 3rd Division had also withdrawn but the 38th held its ground. Fortunately British forces arrived to bolster the line. As the hours wore on the 38th Regiment came under attack from three sides with an active front of some eight miles. At 1630 hours the battalions were ordered to fall back. The 38th had taken 1100 casualties but had inflicted more than 3000 on the enemy. In one spot an American soldier was found dead, his rifle and pistol in hand with 12 Germans lying dead around him.

Further east the 28th Division faced virtually the same situation but was not well enough trained to try the French tactic of slowly giving ground in an effort to inflict maximum casualties on the enemy and thereby drain the momentum of the advance. The Pennsylvanians had been given the simple orders 'Hold at all costs' and they intended to do exactly that. The 28th clung to every foot of ground of their little salient in spite of the enemy artillery, gas and hand-to-hand attacks. The German advance was halted and in words attributed to General Pershing the 28th Division won praise for having 'fought like iron men.' From that they took their title, the 'Iron Division.'

It was now obvious that the German *Friedensturm*, 'Peace Offensive,' would not succeed. The German troops who had been brought from the Russian Front to Western Europe had not turned the tide as the German High Command believed they would. The Americans had arrived in numbers and with fighting abilities which exceeded expectations. The last great German offensive of the war had failed.

It was evident that the Allies now possessed a strong superiority on the front. The Americans had crossed the Marne and were at Château Thierry and French units were on the road to Soissons. The Allies now prepared for their counteroffensive. There were three areas, considered much earlier in the summer, where Marshal Foch intended to direct the Allied offensive in France. In the north at Amiens, where British units were deployed, in the center of the line at Château Thierry, and further south at Saint Mihiel the Germans had pushed three salients into the Allied lines. The largest of these was at Château Thierry. Foch believed that an initial attack in the Soissons area of the salient could trap the German forces, or at least keep them well pinned until a second offensive could be launched to crush them. The idea of a two pronged attack from the west and south was inherently different from previous Allied offensives. It was an attempt not merely to gain ground but also to accomplish the destruction of the enemy's armies.

If the plans were to succeed a maximum effort by the forces on the western face of the salient would be required. That advance was assigned to three divisions, two American and one French. The American 1st and 2nd Divisions were given the company of a French division comprised of French Colonial and Foreign Legion units. These men were seasoned veterans and the Moroccan and Senegalese troops, who made up more than half of the division, were considered some of the fiercest fighters on the entire front. They had a reputation in both the Allied and German camps for refusing to take prisoners unless forced to do so. Persuading them to keep prisoners, even for interrogation, could only be ensured by sending other Allied forces with them to protect the enemy soldiers and escort them to the rear before the Moroccans or Senegalese could kill them.

Right: 'On the Trail of the Hun' by W J Aylward

The 1st Division had been in the line since 5 July at Cantigny. The 2nd Division, which had been pulled from the line for a well-deserved rest, returned to replace the Yankee Division. The officers and men of the 2nd Division were at first unaware that they were to take up an offensive role once again but when it became known that one of the Marine chaplains, Father Murphy, was hearing confessions at the side of the road the men knew that fighting was close at hand. By 17 July the 2nd Division was back in the line preparing for the attack. They were completely ignorant of the enemy's positions and strengths and therefore uncertain of where to place their artillery fire for maximum effect. As they established their lines the Americans were greeted by a sight which few infantry encountered in 1918. French Dragoon cavalry appeared in the line to support the assault. Men and officers alike were fascinated by their arrival and shook their heads in disbelief at the thought of cavalry sent up against German artillery and machine-gun fire. At approximately 2200 hours a torrential downpour began. The men cursed the rain, but were more concerned about the flashes of lightning which lit the area and silhouetted their positions and the French tanks that had also moved forward to participate in the assault. If the German forces sighted these silhouettes through the curtain of rain the advantage of surprise would be lost.

The 1st Division was well established but the 2nd continued to have difficulties. The bulk of their artillery was caught in a massive traffic jam well

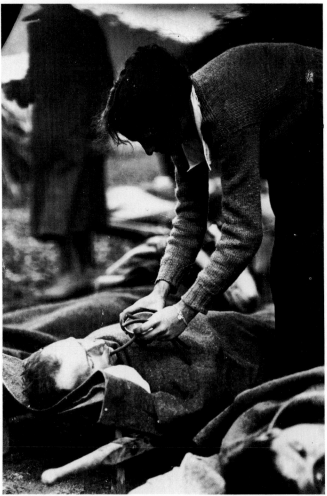

behind the front line. To make the situation worse, the Marine regiments' machine guns were also caught in the congestion and would not arrive by the attack deadline. Attacking without the support of heavy weapons was virtually suicidal, but it was too late to alter the massive planning that had preceded the offensive and the Marines were forced simply to do without.

At 0430 hours on 18 July the Allied counter-offensive began. All four of the 1st Division's regiments, from north to south the 28th, 26th, 16th and 18th, moved forward. The French division was in the center with the 2nd Division's 5th Marine Regiment and 9th and 23rd Infantry Regiments along the line in that order. The 6th Marine Regiment was held in reserve. When the artillery opened fire the German forces were caught completely by surprise and were thrown into confusion. In the first hour of the assault the 1st Division and the French units pushed forward at an astonishingly rapid pace. French tanks easily eliminated pockets of resistance. The 2nd Division, lacking its support fire, began slowly but was soon enjoying the same rapid advance. After taking their first objectives so easily the men were ready to push on. The 1st Division entered an area known as the Missy Ravine and the 2nd Division moved toward the hamlet of Vierzy. The 1st Division had, however, advanced so quickly that their guns could not keep pace and consequently the attack on Missy Ravine was performed without artillery support. After bitter fighting with enormous casualties and the destruction of five French tanks, the Ravine was captured. Other sections of the 1st Division moved on, reaching the Paris–Soissons Road and advancing to the village of Chaudun. Their commanders' tactical abilities were taxed to the limit as they frantically maneuvered companies into the gaps created by the rush forward.

The 2nd Division, although still advancing, was being hampered by German machine-gun positions which kept their village objective just outside their grasp. To make matters worse a group of Senegalese and American troops almost began fighting each other over a group of German prisoners the Americans had captured. The Senegalese troops decided that it was a waste of time and manpower to escort the prisoners to the rear and wanted to rid the Americans of their 'excess baggage' there and then. Another group of Marines captured German troops who turned out to be the personnel of a field kitchen and the Marines were treated to their first hot meal in days. Grabbing sauerkraut in their hands the exhausted Marines ate as they advanced and finally moved into Vierzy after 1900 hours. That night the French Dragoons moved forward and in well-disciplined lines they charged the German positions with sabres drawn. The Americans were awed and disgusted by the charge as they watched the machine guns annihilate the cavalry. Late that night the advance units could see fires burning in the wake of their advance and were heartened by the success of the attack.

However, on the second day of the assault, German forces recovered from their initial shock and the advance could not be so easily continued. By comparison with the first day, the 1st Division was moving at a snail's pace. The gaps in the line forced the division to pause while units attempted to consolidate. German pockets of resistance were taken only after divisional artillery saturated the areas. The 2nd Division advanced to the village of Tigny and although the division repulsed several German counter-attacks its casualty rate rose to more than 4000 killed or wounded. It was obvious that in spite of the division's valiant efforts it could not remain in the line. British troops moved forward as replacements and the 2nd Division moved to the rear for a well-earned respite.

The 1st Division's men were equally exhausted but had to carry on. On the third day of the offensive they and the Moroccans pushed forward to attack the village of Berzy le Sec and the surrounding German positions. Although they gained the high ground around the village, the village itself would not fall. The following day the division tried again. There was heavy resistance and the fatigued 1st took heavy casualties, but through sheer determination they captured Berzy le Sec. By this time the French were beginning to wonder if the 1st Division could stand the stress. It had suffered some 7000 casualties and in four days had pushed faster and farther than any division on the front had ever done. The years of war had accustomed the Allies to moving forward slowly, outflanking the enemy, not engaging head on. However Pershing believed that just as many men died attempting to outflank machine guns as died attacking straight on with rifle and bayonet; and the latter tactic got the job done more quickly. Nonetheless the

counteroffensive on the western perimeter of the salient was losing momentum. If more was to be gained the southern offensive would have to be the one to accomplish it.

At the same time as the attacks by the 1st and 2nd Divisions three American divisions had begun an offensive in the southern sector of the salient. On the westernmost flank the 4th Division, an untried unit, had been brought into line with French regiments. To their right the 26th Yankee Division was positioned at Belleau Wood and the 3rd Division, known now as the (Rock of the) Marne Division, stood to the east at Château Thierry. Their orders were similar to those of the 1st and 2nd Divisions; to drive forward as rapidly as possible, gaining the maximum amount of ground while the attack from the west kept the German Army from relocating reinforcements.

The storm that had drenched the western divisions on the eve of the attack extended to the south and preceded the attack there as well. As the divisions advanced the 4th made steady progress with aid from the intermingled French units. Although the green American troops conducted themselves well, their inexperience led them to bunch up, resulting in higher casualty rates than would otherwise have occurred. The Yankee Division was taking great pride in the rapid pace of its first true offensive. German artillery and machine guns were operating at less

than their normal effectiveness and as the Americans moved forward they were fascinated by the relatively new experience of taking large numbers of German prisoners. The most unusual case of German troops captured occurred when the divisional photographer, who had kept pace with the front line troops to get shots of the action, happened upon a group of German troops. They had never seen the type of camera he carried and when he aimed it at them to take a picture they surrendered, believing he held a new Allied secret weapon. Through the course of the first three days of advance the 4th Division took more than 2000 casualties with the 26th Division's total almost the same. The 3rd Division, which had pushed past Château Thierry had met light resistance and had advanced more than five and one-half miles into the salient.

By the third day of the advance the 3rd Division was meeting much heavier resistance but overcame it on the following day. Its advance continued until after 24 July when it encountered staunch German defenses around Le Charmel. At the same time the 102nd Infantry Regiment of the 26th Division was finding it impossible to maintain its hold on the village of Epieds. Although it fought stubbornly the regiment had taken too many losses to continue the assault. The 102nd was ordered to halt its attack until elements of the 28th Division could be brought

Above: American troops march through Meaux on their way to the front in July 1918.
Above left: Doughboys and WACs relax behind the lines.
Below: A soldier pauses amid the ruins to write a letter.

forward. The units sent had not as yet seen combat and they were shaken by the accounts of the devastating machine-gun fire to which the 26th Division had been exposed and which they would now have to face. At 0615 hours on 24 July they began to advance across the open fields toward Epieds. As each wave moved slowly forward the silence became almost unbearable and the tension mounted as the men awaited the inevitable bursts of German machine-gun fire. They passed the perimeter across which the Yankee Division had not been able to advance and walked into Epieds without a shot being fired. The German units had retired during the night to a new position.

When word of Epieds' capture reached the 26th Division's commander he ordered a general advance to gain as much ground as possible and catch the German forces before they could reestablish defensive positions at Forêt de Fere. It soon became evident that the 26th was too depleted and too weary and the 28th Division's units too green to accomplish the task. They were withdrawn and the 42nd Rainbow Division called in to replace them. The 42nd advanced to Forêt de Fere where they found the German machine guns positioned at a farm outside the wood. The German guns were well sited but the 42nd was launched into an assault nonetheless only to be decimated by the machine-gun fire. Throughout the day and night of 26 July the division continued to press its advance incurring enormous casualties. On the morning of 27 July the assault was renewed only to find that the German units had withdrawn once again.

The German machine-gunners, with their 50 guns, had fallen back to the natural defenses on the far bank of the nearby Ourcq River. Although the river was only five yards wide and waist deep in some areas, it would be enough of an obstacle to the American troops to slow their progress and make them easy prey for the machine guns. On the morning of 28 July the Rainbow Division was again ordered to assault the German positions. The 42nd had been joined by the 3rd and elements of the 28th Division, which had replaced the French units in the center of the line. In the face of horrendous German fire the divisions managed to cross the river but the cost in American lives was staggering. The German units counterattacked in the late afternoon but the Americans displayed a fighting spirit that had gone out of the other Allied armies and held their ground. That evening German aircraft attempted to dislodge the divisions by strafing their positions but still they held. A second German counterattack was dispersed by Allied artillery and the American position was maintained.

In the early hours of 29 July, the 28th and 3rd Divisions advanced, attempting to take Grimpettes Woods, but the German defenders repulsed them three times. The 42nd Division moved toward the town of Sergy, which fell only after two battalions of the 4th Division moved into the area to assist. During the last three days of July the 3rd was retired to be replaced by the 32nd Division, another novice American formation. The 28th and 42nd Divisions continued to plod forward taking enormous casualties while the Allied command spoke lightly of continuing the advance to the Vesle River. The 42nd attacked the German positions north of Sergy while the 28th, bolstered by the fresh though inexperienced 32nd, continued to assault the area around Grimpettes Woods. On 30 July the 28th Division units were taken out of the line leaving the 32nd to try to link the two American advances. On 31 July as the exhausted 42nd continued to creep forward the 32nd took the German defenses at Cierges and Belle Vue.

Finally on 1 August the most important German position in the area, Hill 230, was taken and the German forces were driven back almost to the Vesle. The Allied command took that opportunity to send the entire 4th Division into the line to replace the 42nd. The 4th had been involved in other actions and when it joined the 32nd most of its regiments were only at 75 percent of their normal strength. On 3 August the 4th and 32nd Divisions were ordered to advance to the Vesle but heavy rain on 3 and 4 August slowed their progress and bogged down their artillery support, leaving the American troops exposed to German artillery. By 5 August the Allied artillery had

Above: A group of heavily-
laden American infantrymen
pose with a captured machine
gun.
Above right: American troops
operate a French Chauchat light
machine gun. Although widely
used by the French and
American forces the Chauchat
was a most unsatisfactory design
because the open-sided
magazine tended to allow dirt
into the mechanism.
Left: An empty ambulance in
the ditch, 26 August 1918.
Accidents were common,
especially when an already
muddy road had been damaged
by shell fire.

moved forward, relieving some of the pressure. The
Vesle was reached and by the afternoon of 6 August
units had actually managed to cross the river in
certain sectors. On that afternoon elements of the
28th and 3rd Divisions were returned to the line.
Within two days the Iron Division had crossed the
Vesle and taken the village of Fismette. On 9 August
the 4th Division advanced to the village of Bazoches
but was repulsed by German air attacks.

For the next 10 days the American advance halted,
although pressure was maintained by artillery and
infantry fire. On 19 August, with American reinforcements in the line Bazoches was taken and then the
fortress of Château du Diable fell, forcing the German units to pull back. Just as it began to appear that
the German forces would have to withdraw behind
the Aisne River they launched an awesome counterattack on 27 August. Bazoches was lost and two full
companies of the 28th Division were isolated and
eliminated at Fismette. However, by the following
morning, the American and Allied forces were reorganizing and moving forward in several sectors,
especially near Juvigny. The American forces which
had been thrown back to the Vesle from Bazoches also
advanced once again. All along the front Allied forces,
such as the British at Amiens, were slowly advancing,
noticing as they did so that the German infantry had
more young boys and old men in the ranks than had
previously been seen. Germany was definitely suffer-
ing and by the last day of August the Château Thierry
salient had been eliminated and the German armies
were pulling back. The Allied command looked forward to continuing its offensive in the months ahead.

4 WAR IN THE SKIES

The airplane made its military debut during World War I but the United States was not prepared for the application of this relatively new innovation. Before the war the airplane was seen as an unpredictable plaything and the US War Department certainly viewed military aviation as a lunatic scheme. The governments of Europe, particularly in France and Russia, had responded enthusiastically to the Wright Brothers' successful mastery of the dream of flight, aware of its wide potential. The American government and the Department of the Army appeared smugly satisfied when a demonstration aircraft piloted by Orville Wright and one of the Army's first pilots, Lieutenant Thomas Selfridge, crashed from a height of 75 feet. Lieutenant Selfridge was killed and Wright was injured, confirming the War Department's belief that flight was an unpredictable menace. This opinion was heavily weighted by the fact that the primary use envisioned for the airplane was in reconnaissance, previously the preserve of the cavalry. The airplane was thus a threat to this prestigious section of the army.

Congress agreed that aviation in its current form had no practical military value but was pressured into appropriating funds for a limited program involving aircraft. These aircraft were attached to the Signal Corps which received an inventory of five airplanes, three balloons and six pilots. Lieutenant Henry 'Hap' Arnold, who would later command the US air forces in World War II, was one of the best American pilots although he had logged no more than 29 hours of flight time. Three years later the United States was doing little more with aircraft and by 1914 the air force had increased by only one airplane and nine pilots with a total budget of $125,000. At that time France had 260 aircraft, with 191 pilots, and had allocated the equivalent of $7,500,000 to the development of an air force. Germany had 46 aircraft, 52 pilots and had designated $5,000,000 to the program.

The full potential of aircraft in reconnaissance became clear as the war in Europe escalated. In a relatively short time an airplane could enter enemy territory, detect strengths and weaknesses and then return to report the findings. Pilots could land to report personally on their findings or drop canisters containing maps marked with designated symbols to

Above: Henry 'Hap' Arnold, one of the first American pilots, seen here early in his career. Right: Pilots of the Lafayette Escadrille with their lion mascots. From left; Hall, Thaw, Hill, Marr, Peterson, Lufbery, Rockwell, Bridgman and a French officer.

indicate enemy positions. This practice gave quick, reliable information to the military headquarters. Aerial photography could give commanders in the field first-hand information on enemy fortification and fieldworks enabling them to plan their tactics accordingly. Photography also helped to confirm which supply routes were heavily used and where reserves were concentrated. Aircraft also made excellent artillery observers.

As the war developed it was only a matter of time before one side or the other recognized the full capabilities of the airplane as an offensive weapon, able to drop gas or explosives on enemy troops without endangering friendly units in the attempt. However, the US War Department continued to view the airplane with disdain and adventurous young Americans who would gladly have become pilots in the States packed up and went off to France.

On 20 April 1916, while the United States still clung to its neutralist ideals, seven Americans formed what would become one of the most famous, romanticized units of the war in Europe. Originally entitled the 'Escadrille Americaine' they were the first Americans to participate in the war, though they fought under the flag and in the aircraft of the French. Of the original seven: Norman Prince, Bill Thaw, Victor Chapman, Kiffin Rockwell, Jim McConnell, Elliot Cowdin and Bert Hall, only Hall would survive the war unscathed. The men were not happy with the unit's title and searched for something with a little more flair. They finally decided on the 'Escadrille Lafayette' saying that their part in the war was in some small way a repayment of the debt owed to that great French general and hero of the American Revolutionary War.

In a very brief time the squadron became famous, largely through the efforts of an American doctor, Edmund Gros. His contact with the men made him realize that publication of their exploits would serve as excellent propaganda to bring America closer to cooperation with the Allies. In the States he made certain that their role in the war was well documented and publicized. They were depicted as modern-day knights, jousting in the skies, fighting their own war high above the muddy trenches. Their esprit de corps and the mystique that surrounded them gave the Lafayette Escadrille a special appeal to intelligent young men looking for adventure. Although the propaganda promoted the romantic image of the squadron, there is no denying that those early aviators were indeed a special breed of men.

Flight was not all glamor and glory. As men arrived in France intent on joining the Lafayette Escadrille the first aircraft they encountered was not an airplane at all but a fuselage with an engine, instruments and

Above: The identity card of an officer of the AEF.
Left: Sergeant Soubiran of the Lafayette Escadrille poses in front of a Nieuport scout at Cachy Airdrome during the British Somme offensive in 1916. When the US joined the war Soubiran transferred to the US Air Service and later commanded the 103rd Aero Squadron, formerly the Lafayette Escadrille.

stubby wings mounted in a static position. In it the student would learn how to start and stop the engine properly, how to read the gauges and generally be convinced through exposure and instruction that such a machine made of metal, wood and cloth held together with bolts and wire could indeed fly. Descriptions of the principles of flight were minimal. In fact, close examination of those early aircraft, coupled with the details of their instability, seems to bear witness to claims that it was the enthusiasm and faith of those early aviators and not the mechanical genius of aircraft designers and builders which kept the machines airborne.

After the orientation was completed the instructors introduced the students to 'the Penguins.' These aircraft were so dubbed because they had short wings and were incapable of flight. In a Penguin the student learned to taxi on the airstrip and gained a knowledge of ground control. Their insufficient wing span was intended to keep over-zealous students from becom-

Balloons were used extensively by all the combatants in World War I.
Above: An accident in training at Fort Sill, Oklahoma.
Both left: Balloon operations in France.

ing airborne, but there were many cases where the students managed to hop the aircraft five or more feet into the air. This horrified the instructors and the mechanics who had to keep the Penguins operable. Neither was it uncommon for the enthusiastic students to become so absorbed in their flight fantasies that they crashed into buildings, walls, and each other.

If by some miracle the student survived his instruction and became proficient with his craft, he graduated to Virages. These aircraft were designed to give the novice aviators a chance to become accustomed to actual flight, to practice taking off and landing and to learn the principles of maneuvering an aircraft in flight. Students were told to keep an altitude of 50–100 feet and to practice gentle turns around the airfield. The Virages were of light construction but flexible enough to forgive an awkward, tight turn without ripping apart, which was not uncommon for aircraft of the period. That characteristic of flexibility produced tales of pilots making tight banks only to look over their shoulders to see the fuselage and tail twist with the maneuver. Nose dives, flips and crashes were all part of learning to land the aircraft. The men explained that while flying was a glorious experience the sudden stop at the end could ruin the day. One student of the Escadrille actually crashed three different aircraft in the same day. Cuts, bruises and broken bones were commonplace. Efforts were made to minimize the dangers and seatbelts were installed in the airplanes to hold pilots in during accidents. Safety helmets were also supplied but the men complained that helmets came in only two sizes, too big and too small.

With the principles learned the men were sent on cross-country flights to develop navigational skills. The men claimed to enjoy this phase of training best. They would go to great lengths to become lost and forced to land near the chateau or farm of a friendly French family, preferably one with beautiful daughters. Daughters or not they were always greeted with warm generosity. The Lafayette Escadrille became noted for such escapades and it convinced their instructors that they were too frivolous to make good fighters. The truth was that the American aviators were still caught up in the naive enjoyment of flying. They had not yet grown weary and somber as had their French and British counterparts. For them the adventure was new and they sought to maintain the innocence of their role for as long as possible.

The final phase of instruction was actual combat experience and the development of the maneuvering and acrobatic skills that combat demanded. It was then that the harsh realities of flight became apparent. In training serious injuries or deaths could be rationalized as stupid accidents. In combat with enemy aircraft in pursuit and in aircraft that were fast and intolerant of the slightest mistake, the dangers were both startling and finite. A very quick death could come from a burst of enemy fire or from a second's misjudgment in flight. It was not uncommon for the aircraft they flew simply to disintegrate in mid-air. The strain of repeated flight and structural fatigue meant that it was not unusual for a pilot to initiate a maneuver only to have the wings or tail section separate from the aircraft, or the fabric skin rip away from the wings. Fires in the aircraft were also prevalent. The morbid joke of the aviators was, 'don't worry about the crash, the fire will kill you first.' There were many documented reports of friends and enemies leaping from their burning airplanes. Glory and horror were inseparable facets of the infant field of aviation.

As the fame of the Lafayette Escadrille rose and its

exploits were magnified, the United States government was persuaded by public demand to make a commitment to the development of aviation. The War Department and Congress finally acknowledged the extent of the possibilities. Acts were passed and funds appropriated to bring the United States up to date in aviation. As America became increasingly involved in the war American squadrons began to form and American pilots no longer trained in France but at Kelly's Field, Texas or near San Diego, California or on Long Island, New York. In the frantic rush to form squadrons it was not uncommon for student pilots to be sent to airfields for instruction only to discover weeks later that someone had forgotten to send the airplanes as well. The excitement created by the Lafayette Escadrille was infectious and men of all segments of society enlisted. One class of student aviators consisted of a stockbroker, a farmer, a race-car driver, a salesman and a pianist, all seeking the adventure of flight. American-built Curtiss JN4D 'Jenny' biplanes were widely used for training.

The first American combat squadron was the 95th Aero Squadron. When they arrived in France they were supplied with French Nieuports that had no machine guns, nor was gunnery training mentioned to the men. Undaunted by the lack of weapons these aviators flew reconnaissance missions over hostile territory unarmed. After several weeks of operations the Allied command challenged the squadron's effectiveness, for although there were reports of aerial engagements, with one American pilot lost, there were no reports of any enemy shot down by the 95th. The

American commander returned a report stating that they would be most happy to shoot down the enemy as soon as the Allied command saw fit to supply them with machine guns. When the report reached headquarters the squadron was immediately pulled from the line and sent to the rear for gun fitting and gunnery instruction.

The unarmed actions of the 95th 'Hat in the Ring' Squadron were foolish but the adventurous aviators were determined to make a mark for themselves. Their pride and courage was the beginning of the American aviation tradition. Men such as Lieutenant Eddie Rickenbacker, former race-car driver and personal chauffeur to General Pershing, served with the squadron. Rickenbacker would become America's leading ace with 26 enemy aircraft shot down. Raoul Lufbery, the oldest pilot at age 28, who like many others transferred to the 95th from the Lafayette Escadrille, and Douglas Campbell who was America's first ace, helped develop the aura of American wartime aviation. A children's magazine called *War Aces* described the exploits of such men and led young boys into the aviation field. Through *War Aces* and other publicity the aviator's careers were followed by the American people. One of the most colorful figures was Frank Luke of the 27th Aero Squadron. Known as

the 'balloon buster' for his daring attacks on German observation balloons, Luke's commander gave him permission to perform missions alone because his recklessness made him dangerous to fly with. One man who would fly in partnership with Luke was Lieutenant Joe Wehner. Together they accumulated a high score of balloons and enemy aircraft destroyed. Wehner was killed aiding Luke when under the attack of seven enemy aircraft. Shortly thereafter Luke went out on a mission and was never seen again. When the commander of the 27th Aero Squadron, Major Harold Hartney, sent word of Luke's death to his family in Arizona it was discovered that Luke's mother never even knew her son was in Europe.

By the time the war ended more than 650 American aviators had seen action with 781 confirmed kills of enemy aircraft to their credit.

5 THE FINAL OFFENSIVES

The desperate need for reinforcements had broken Pershing's iron hold on the commitment of American forces, giving Marshal Foch control over their deployment in the spring and summer of 1918. On 10 August Pershing was officially given command of the American First Army Europe and he set about reorganizing and consolidating his divisions. Pershing was determined to put a halt to the piecemeal deployment of American troops in positions which made them little more than cannon fodder, sacrificed to spare the so called 'essential veteran' French and British divisions. Pershing's nightmares of Allied drives fighting to the last American were dispelled as he took command.

With the American army now at his command Pershing sought to implement an offensive which was strictly American from beginning to end. Although American divisions had seen a great deal of action they had operated as support or to take the brunt of German firepower preceding French or British units in the line. Pershing wanted to prove that an American army could function as well if not better than its Allied counterparts. The point that Pershing chose for an American operation was the salient at St Mihiel, the farthest south of the three created by the earlier German offensives. After crushing the salient the Americans would advance north to the city of Metz, capturing the town and its vital railhead. Pershing and Foch immediately began to argue about just exactly what the Americans would be permitted to do in the projected attack.

As the Allied offensive in the Château Thierry salient began to wind down Foch suggested a limited American attack supporting French units, whose only goal would be to eliminate the St Mihiel salient. Pershing strongly opposed the plan on the grounds that Foch wanted to scatter the American divisions among the French. The American command was tired of its troops being thrown into areas that they described as 'meat grinders' while French units took avenues of less resistance or moved in to perform the mopping-up operations. The French like the British had been at war for a long time, but Pershing considered their tactics as nothing more than a means to acquire the most glory at the Americans' expense as repayment for their years of fighting.

Pershing would no longer argue the issue and called Foch's bluff. He informed the French commander that unless he was willing to concede that Americans could fight as an independent army he would not permit the American divisions to engage in any further action. Foch protested vehemently but Pershing was prepared to carry out his threat to withdraw American divisions from the line, returning them to their training areas, until the dispute was resolved. Foch was forced to acquiesce. American forces would no longer be divided and would, unless otherwise directed by Pershing, fight as an independent army. Although the aim would be to take the St Mihiel salient Foch would not agree to the advance to Metz. He had other plans in mind for the American forces.

American and French divisions now converged on the 600 square mile salient. As they did so Pershing organized his divisions into two corps. On the southeast perimeter of the salient he placed the US I Corps

immobile while the Americans made their rendezvous.

As the Allied forces attempted to move quietly forward into the area their superiority on the line mounted. More than 3000 artillery pieces were brought forward and 270 French light tanks added their weight to support the offensive. Air raids against the German positions were planned to be conducted prior to the advance. When the Allied forces were finally assembled they numbered a quarter of a million men, more than 200,000 of whom were Americans. The German forces in the salient, com-

of the 2nd, 5th, 9th, and 82nd Divisions. The latter three divisions were relatively new and had little line experience. Major General Hunter Liggett took command of I Corps. To the left of I Corps Pershing formed the US IV Corps using 1st and 42nd Divisions and the mid-West draftee division, the 89th, placing General Dickman in command. Farther north the American 26th Yankee Division and the French 15th Division combined to form the US V Corps, General George Cameron commanding. French divisions lay around St Mihiel itself, separating V Corps from the other two. The I Corps' assignment was to push into the salient with the town of Thiaucourt as its objective. The 26th Division on the western perimeter and IV Corps on the southern perimeter were to push ahead of the French to rendezvous at Vigneulles. In accomplishing that maneuver the Americans hoped to trap the majority of German forces in that area of the salient. At St Mihiel the French were to maintain slow, constant pressure to keep the German units

manded by General Fuchs, were outnumbered by approximately three to one.

At 0100 hours on 12 September the first Allied shells began to fall on the enemy defenses. A rainstorm had broken just prior to the attack and the veteran soldiers of the 1st and 2nd Divisions began to joke about the fact that the Hun should know by now when the Americans would be attacking – it always rained. At 0500 hours the order was given to go over the top and the American corps advanced. Although German resistance was staunch in some areas, by and large it had been eliminated by the combination of Allied artillery and air strikes. Not even Mon Sec, the most dreaded of the German strongholds, presented a problem in the advance. German prisoners were taken en masse. The 89th Division took more prisoners than casualties and in one instance a sergeant captured 300 prisoners with an empty pistol. As he herded them to the rear he was halted for more than 30 minutes while he attempted to convince his platoon commander that

the Germans were in fact prisoners and not an enemy counterattack.

On the afternoon of 12 September American cavalry was brought forward to reconnoiter the area but was quickly withdrawn in the face of enemy machine-gun fire. Although the cavalry performed its role with honor and distinction it had become obvious that in this new warfare, with massive fire-power being brought to bear, there was no longer a place for mounted soldiers on the field of battle. Traditionalists in the military would miss the glory of the cavalry charge, but in modern warfare that glory had been converted to a suicidal gesture.

By nightfall on the first day most of the initial objectives had been taken but the 26th Division, which was to link with IV Corps at Vigneulles, was still 10 miles away. At Pershing's personal command the 26th marched throughout the night to accomplish the rendezvous. By dawn on 13 September the towns of Vigneulles and Thiaucourt were under American control and at 0600 the 26th Division closed the gap, trapping the German forces between there and St Mihiel. Along the front some 15,000 German troops and 440 heavy weapons had been captured. American casualties were amazingly light. In fact the entire operation would claim only slightly more than a 3 percent casualty rate from the American units. The success could not have come at a better time. General Pershing's birthday was 13 September and he claimed that it was the happiest he had had for a very long time.

For the next three days the American and French forces cleared the salient of German resistance,

Above & above right: Two photographs taken within a few moments of each other. Above, men of the 111th Infantry amuse their buddies in the newly captured town of Thiaucourt and above right, performers and audience run for cover as a German bombardment begins.
Far right, top: The US Army transport *Logan* arrives in Vladivostock Harbor during the Allied intervention in the Russian Revolution.
Right: An ammunition wagon stuck on the muddy road near Beaumont Ridge in the St Mihiel salient, 15 September 1918.

establishing a new front line. They continued to move north and east but Foch halted the operation before it could capture Metz. As stated earlier he had other plans and shifted the focus from the salient to a drive from the Meuse River to the Argonne Forest. Foch's battle schedule gave Pershing only 10 days to maneuver his army and reestablish it at a new location for the advance on the Argonne. The St Mihiel offensive had indeed been 'a stroll at St Mihiel' when compared to what the Americans were about to face.

In those mid-September days the wider events of the war were extremely encouraging. In diplomatic

Central Powers, and to aid the White Russian Armies against the Red. The Japanese had also begun to appear suspiciously interested in areas of the Siberian/Chinese border. Each of these factors contributed to American forces being dispatched to Archangel on the White Sea and to Vladivostok. The entire operation cost a great many American lives, some 2000 at Archangel alone, and in the long term did little more than incite the new government of Russia against the Allies. However, in the light of events on a global scale it was becoming obvious that of the Central Powers it was Germany which would hold out the longest, and equally obvious that if Germany chose to prolong the war it would soon be doing so alone.

The Americans had just won a major victory. Allied morale soared and the Allied command had been made confident of the Americans' combat abilities. All along the front, from the North Sea to Verdun Foch called for one last great offensive, which he was convinced would break the German armies' will. The Americans were to contribute to this with their attack on the Argonne Forest. Pershing realized that in the time allotted him for the assault preparations he could not maneuver his veteran divisions to the primary point of attack and would be forced to send in green troops to execute the assault. As Pershing reviewed the plans and the units available for the assault he became increasingly worried. The available American forces were not merely amateurs. Their experience was so limited that they could barely be classified as soldiers. But there was really nothing Pershing could do. Although the situation seemed precarious Pershing was confident that the new divisions would acquit themselves as well as so many novice soldiers had done before them.

circles Austria-Hungary was sending out peace feelers. The fact that the US had succeeded in transporting more than 1,500,000 men to Europe in a matter of months was having its effects. Elsewhere the Allies were achieving great successes. In the Middle East the British were winning their war against the Turks in Palestine. In another area an Allied sortie into affairs on the Eastern Front was not as successful. The British command decided that opportunities had been presented to aid the Czechoslovakian forces in their efforts against Austria-Hungary, to reopen an Eastern Front against the

The overall strategy in which the Americans were to be involved consisted of a combined offensive along the entire Front. If the Americans could break through the two-mile line between the Argonne and the Meuse, and if they could continue forward to the city of Sedan, then it was believed that a large contingent of German troops would be trapped with no avenue of retreat between the Americans and the Ardennes. The primary French and British offensives would then move forward and crush the German Army. The allegedly impenetrable Ardennes were rejected by the Allied command as a means of retreat for the German forces and the commanders agreed that once the Americans took Sedan, considered the only valid escape or reinforcement route for the massive numbers of German troops, the German Army in France would be easily destroyed.

The principal problem with this strategy was that it was based on a fallacy. The Ardennes, though thick forest, had several adequate roads and rail lines over which troops might pass with little danger of congestion hindering the speed of their movement. Therefore even before the last great offensive was begun it had little chance of achieving its ultimate goal of trapping and destroying the German Army. Another fallacy in the plans of the Allied Command lay in the belief that when the American Army attacked the German strategic reserve of 25–30 divisions would be pulled from the support of the main front to counter the Americans in the Argonne Forest region. A German relocation of troops to maintain their avenues of retreat would weaken the main front, allowing Allied troops all along the line to push forward more easily. In the event the German command realized that there was no need for panic and maintained their flexible defenses, dropping slowly back or shifting troops along the front whenever and wherever needed. Unfortunately for the American forces the foundation of the strategic battle plan in effect existed only in the minds of the Allied Commanders.

The American Army was regrouped establishing three corps along their sector of the front. On the extreme left flank at the Argonne was Major General Liggett's I Corps. This corps now comprised three divisions. The 77th Division was made up of draftees from New York. It was an odd choice to send headlong into the dense forest as the majority of the men were from inner city areas. On their right was the veteran 28th Iron Division. Their primary tasks were to advance up the Aire River Valley and to sustain the cohesion of the corps, keeping contact with the 77th and the 35th Division, the corps' right flank division. The green 35th Division had the line of least resistance but the division had acquired a poor reputation in Europe. Internal strife between the Kansas and Missouri National Guard and the regular officers of the division had created what amounted to a feud. The

National Guardsmen knew their staff and felt that their officers were capable of managing the division. They resented the fact that regular officers were consistently placed in key positions in their division. This attachment of regular officers to the National Guard was common practice but the men and officers of the 35th refused to accept it and the rift continued to widen. It was the consensus of the National Guard officers that the regulars were nothing more than spies sent by Pershing to gather enough detrimental information on them to have the entire staff replaced. Conversely the regular officers resented the fact that most of the National Guard officers had received their rank and position not through military service but through their political influence in their home states. The underlying turmoil within the 35th Division brought its battlefield ability into serious question.

East of I Corps lay Major General Cameron's V Corps. His corps was composed of the 91st Division on the left, the 37th Division holding the center, and the 79th Division on the far right flank. Cameron, a veteran of several offensives, could not help but be discouraged by the men he was given. All three divisions were made up of draftees from throughout America and although they were able bodied men with an excellent esprit they had never seen combat. Cameron knew that on the line nothing could replace experience and he privately wondered how much of his corps he would lose as that experience was gained.

Farthest east was III Corps, commanded by Major General Robert Bullard. Unlike I and V Corps, whose staffs had directed other battles and had established and adequate chains of command which knew their way around the front, III Corps' staff was about to participate in its first engagement. The veteran 4th Division and the 80th and 33rd Divisions formed the corps. Although the latter two divisions had precious little combat experience they had served on the front in northern sectors with the British Army and had some idea of what they could expect in the impending offensive.

Of the nine divisions assembled to lead the American First Army's attack only two, the 28th and 4th, had worthwhile combat experience. In spite of the optimism expressed by the Allied and American commands there had to be some question about their ability to drive 30 miles into enemy territory. Ahead of them lay three major German defensive lines. Two were located on the front itself but the third, the Hindenburg Line, would be a formidable obstacle to overcome. Other veteran American divisions including the 1st, 2nd, and 42nd were to the rear, resting and refitting so that Pershing could apply them when the American advance reached the Hindenburg Line. Once the green divisions had broken through it would be the responsibility of the veteran divisions to exploit the advantage and maintain the momentum of the advance. Apparently Pershing had come to believe in

Right: An American tank unit advances along a forest road near Boureilles on 26 September 1918 during the Meuse-Argonne Battle. The tanks are of the Renault FT type.
Below: An American 14-inch railway gun in action near Bategcourt on the same day as the tank advance shown at right.

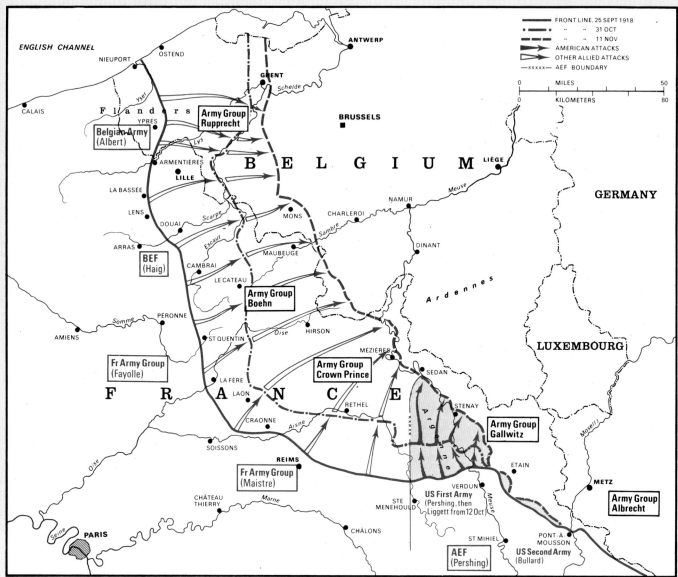

FRONT LINE, 25 SEPT 1918
"   "   "   31 OCT
"   "   "   11 NOV
AMERICAN ATTACKS
OTHER ALLIED ATTACKS
-xxxxx- AEF BOUNDARY

MILES
KILOMETERS

Foch's notion of sending inexperienced troops in to do the initial dirty work, for he later pointed out that there 'would not have been any point to wasting precious veteran lives' in what promised to be a bloody endeavor.

On the evening of 25 September 1918 the American divisions took their positions in preparation for the attack. As usual each man carried his 200 rounds of ammunition, two cans of corned beef, six boxes of hard bread and a one quart canteen. On this occasion however, many of the novice American soldiers had put wine in their canteens. They had no veterans around to warn that in the heat of battle the wine had a marked tendency to turn a man's stomach. Later, when the primary concern should have been dealing with the German machine guns these men would be focussing too much of their attention on the illness the wine produced.

At 0230 hours on 26 September the artillery began the attack with a devastating barrage followed by shelling with smoke canisters. When the firing finally ceased the men moved forward into the blanket of

smoke that the artillery had created. Although the smoke cloud hindered their progress they soon realized that it also hid them from the German machine-gunners. The Americans were almost on top of the German defenses before the enemy troops realized what was happening and the initial attacks proceeded extremely well.

In III Corps' sector the 33rd Division moved forward quickly taking its first objective along the Meuse River. The 80th Division encountered little resistance and continued moving north. The 4th Division's veterans used compasses and plotted a direct course. By 1230 hours they had pushed all the way to Nantillois, several miles into German territory. Their drive was so successful and the division in such good order with so few casualties that Pershing wanted to send III Corps on a swing to take the primary objective of the high ground surrounding Montfaucon but the other two divisions were scattered and Pershing was forced to call a five-hour halt to reconsolidate the corps. In so doing III Corps lost its initial advantage of surprise. The German forces had time to recover and withdraw to a flexible defensive stance. More importantly German reserves were brought forward to strengthen their lines.

In any case Montfaucon was the objective assigned to V Corps. The 79th Division had been forced to withdraw from Bois de Malancourt and was stalled, wandering in the Cuisy Woods sector of their front. On it's left flank the 37th Division found the going much easier. There the Allied artillery had done its job well and the division met little resistance. The 91st Division had advanced to the outskirts of the village of Epinonville, which meant that Montfaucon was outflanked on its left by V Corps and on its right by III Corps. Once the 79th Division reorganized and moved forward Montfaucon should fall.

The I Corps' progress through the Argonne was much more difficult but it advanced steadily and gave no indication that it would inhibit or delay the offensive. The 35th Division was halted for several hours outside the well-defended village of Cheppy but French tanks came to its aid and by dusk the division had reached Very. The 'city boys' of the 77th Division advanced through the forest growth of the Argonne with a pace that surprised the veterans of the 28th.

Left: The map shows the Allied advance from 25 September until the Armistice.
Below: A machine-gun platoon of the 80th Division advances.

In the early hours of 27 September French tanks caught up with the advance of the 79th Division and together they took the Bois de Malancourt at 1145 hours after a costly night battle. However, by the end of that second day the advance had begun to lose momentum. Most of the French artillery and tanks were bogged down in the mud that the rain of the first two days had created and the infantry were forced to halt while the heavy support reached its positions. The men were exhausted by the terrain, the enemy obstacles they had faced and the effort that they had put forth to reach their objectives. The divisional commanders realized that their men needed food and rest if they were to continue. One colonel of the 37th Division was so angered by the pressure to advance that he threatened to contact Pershing himself with the message that he refused to push his men any farther until they got some sleep and a hot meal.

By the morning of 29 September the condition of the divisions was beginning to be markedly apparent. Montfaucon could not be taken without the support of the artillery and tanks and the 37th Division had taken a beating attempting to advance through the Bois de Montfaucon. The 35th Division, though an extreme case because of its internal problems, was a primary example of how disorganized and exhausted the divisions were. Orders were issued to make yet another advance on the 29th to Exermont. Although some units succeeded in gaining their objectives,

disorganization kept reinforcements from aiding them. They fought bravely but German counter-attacks began to take their toll. Afraid of being isolated and possibly surrounded in the village the units withdrew. Including the Exermont attack, the 35th Division had taken 8000 casualties and would have to be replaced. The 35th Division clearly illustrated that the time was drawing near for Pershing to withdraw the novice divisions and move his veterans forward.

The 1st Division moved forward to replace the 35th, with the 3rd Division relieving the 79th and the 32nd Division replacing the 37th. Although the green divisions had not remained in the field as long as Pershing had originally intended they did succeed in breaking through two defensive lines and had almost captured Montfaucon. As the veteran divisions advanced the 77th Division (I Corps) was still cutting its way through the Argonne Forest. On 1 October the division was ordered to increase the pace of its advance. Leading the way was the 1st Battalion of the 308th Infantry Regiment, commanded by Major Charles Whittlesey. As the battalion moved forward it was concerned about its exposed position and about the reliability of the supporting units on its flanks. On the right, though out of sight and often out of communication, was the 308th's sister regiment the 307th. However, on the left flank were French units.

These particular units had done their part in the recent past to give black American soldiers a bad reputation along the line. American Negro Brigades, segregated from the American First Army, had been attached to the French and had unjustly been accused of breaking in a previous engagement. In fact the black troops' position was intolerable. They fell under the command of French officers who issued orders in French that they could not understand and were repeatedly sent forward to clear a path through which French troops could then march gloriously once the worst fighting was over. It was amazing that the black troops managed to fight at all, not that they should lose heart and flee.

As Whittlesey's battalion moved due north they encountered a defended region that had all the earmarks of a death trap. Whittlesey decided to push his troops toward the high ground of Hill 198, taking the path of least resistance. After successfully maneuvering his battalion, and knowing that close support was near in the form of the 2nd Battalion, 308th Regiment, Whittlesey's men crested the hill then moved down the slopes to Charlevaux Brook. As the 1st Battalion crossed the antiquated foot bridge German machine guns opened fire. They were trapped in the valley. Steep banks and forest surrounded the battalion, both well fortified and strongly manned. Whittlesey

attempted to send messengers to the rear and flanks requesting assistance. The 307th Regiment responded but by the morning of 2 October only one company had reached Whittlesey's position. The rest were lost in the dark forest or intercepted by enemy fire. Just as the company arrived, adding their weight to Whittlesey's 575 remaining men, the German forces closed the gap isolating the battalion completely. By 0930 hours German mortars, artillery and grenades were pounding the American position and German reinforcements were being added to the encirclement.

It was obvious that they were surrounded and the men of Whittlesey's command spent the day and night of 3 October fending off German assaults. By the next morning there were less than 500 men left and food and ammunition supplies were running short. At divisional headquarters it was decided that as they could not get infantry forward to relieve the battalion they would saturate the surrounding area with artillery fire. This attempt to aid the men of the 1st Battalion ended in disaster. The artillery, which only had an approximate idea of Whittlesey's position, dropped their barrage not on the enemy but on the American troops. The bombardment continued for almost four hours, stopping only after the battalion's last homing pigeon reached divisional command with

a message reporting it and the battalion's coordinates which ended, 'For Heaven's sake, stop it.'

On the morning of 5 October the perimeter around the battalion was closing. German snipers harassed the American troops. Their food was gone and although rain had provided drinking water the men resorted to eating the birdseed that the pigeon handler had left. As they waited helplessly an American reconnaissance pilot flew over the area and spotted the battalion. He could also see the German forces massing for an attack. The pilot promptly dropped signal flares on the enemy positions. Divisional artillery, able to range on the flares, bombarded the German forces. As the barrage began the American troops took cover and soon a cheer went up as the German forces scattered.

By 6 October only 275 men of Whittlesey's battalion were left. There was no food and although Allied aircraft tried to drop food and ammunition to the men most of it landed outside their reach. German snipers laid out the food as bait, killing any soldier who tried to reach it. The men decided that several volunteers should attempt to go for aid. Of them, Private Abe Krotoshinsky eventually reached the American lines. However, on 6 October the American 1st and 2nd Divisions were breaking through the lines and the

German forces around Whittlesey's battalion knew that if they were going to eliminate the pocket they would have to do it quickly.

On 7 October the German commander called for the Americans to surrender but Whittlesey refused. In answer the German flame throwers were brought forward to sweep the area. Still the men held. On 8 October Lieutenant Tillman's Company B of the 307th Regiment arrived led by Private Krotoshinsky. There were only 194 men left in what had become known as the 'Lost Battalion,' though the men later said that they preferred to be called 'Surrounded.'

What had happened to the 1st Battalion was preceded and repeated countless times on the American battlefields. The men of the 1st Battalion were not unique but they were an excellent example of the determination with which even the greenest of American soldiers faced overwhelming odds. The aftermath of the 1st Battalion action also provides a grim reminder of the horror of war. For his leadership in the gallant defense Charles Whittlesey was promoted to Lieutenant Colonel and awarded the Congressional Medal of Honor. His men and those who knew him said that the mild-mannered New Englander was never the same after Charlevaux, but he never told anyone exactly what was bothering him. Three years later on a vacation cruise bound for Cuba he jumped over the ship's rail to his death.

Elsewhere on the American First Army's Front a second major thrust began at 0525 hours on 4 October. As the attacks pushed forward most of the divisions reached their objectives quickly though with more casualties than had been expected. German artillery had been brought to the far side of the Meuse and the German lines reinforced during the lull. On 5 October the 26th Regiment of the 1st Division broke through and captured a strategic point at Hill 269, only to discover that the German defenders were gone. They were not able to exploit the free path they had been given as the remainder of the division was caught totally off-guard and out of position to pursue the advantage.

For the next few days the German forces continued to pull back slowly in an orderly, flexible defense and it became apparent that if the offensive to extend the Allied sphere of control was to succeed the German positions in the Argonne Forest would have to be taken. That task was assigned to the 1st, 28th and 82nd 'All American' Division. In the advance of the 82nd one of its men gained a reputation as the 'war's greatest civilian soldier.' While on patrol Alvin Cullum York and eight other troops were caught and pinned down by German machine-gun fire. York, who grew up in the mountains of Tennessee and had become an expert shot hunting small game, put his marksmanship to good use as one by one he eliminated the German gunners. His deadly accurate fire also stopped a German counterattack. When the incident

had ended York had killed 25 and captured 132 German soldiers, for which he was awarded the Congressional Medal of Honor. Oddly enough before his induction York had petitioned his draft board for status as a conscientious objector on religious grounds, saying that it was only after 'a lot of prayer and soul searching' that he entered the line at all. Twenty years later York would again serve his country in World War II as a counselor for young men who wished to be declared conscientious objectors.

While the 82nd Division was earning its reputation the 33rd Division moved across the Meuse River to take the heights beyond, where the German artillery batteries were positioned. Although French and American divisions joined forces at the village of Grand Pré, they could go no further and it was apparent that the advance would stall once again. In the midst of the assault the American First Army underwent yet another drastic change. The army was

Left: Sergeant York pictured in February 1919 on the hillside where he won his Medal of Honor.
Below right: Rapid fire from an American 75mm gun, October 1918.
Below: The German machine-gun post which held the advance at Grand Pré seen after its eventual capture.

divided in two. West of the Meuse the forces became the American First Army, commanded by Major General Hunter Liggett. East of the river the Second Army was formed under the command of Major General Robert Bullard. The loss of momentum in the American drive prompted Pershing to take this step. The French and British offensives were gaining their objectives and literally rolling up the German defenders. British forces, with support from the American 30th and 27th Divisions, had not only broken through the German front lines but had cut a hole through the Hindenburg Line with open country now lying before them. With the Hindenburg Line broken the German forces were in a bad position. The German command not only intended to use the line for its winter defense, but had hoped to come to a peace settlement while still holding that commanding defensive position.

Pershing wanted no more excuses. He wanted the American objectives taken immediately. With two armies operating independently to achieve the American objectives the First Army on the left would strike and once its drive gained momentum the Second Army would move forward, thus trapping the enemy between them. For the remainder of October the

Americans reorganized. The main combat arena had shifted momentarily from the battlefields to the American staff rooms. General Liggett, considered to possess the most initiative and to be America's best field tactician, opposed Pershing's two-pronged-offense theory. Liggett argued that the most productive course would be to drive a broad wedge in the center of the German line. Such an assault would outflank Bois de Bourgogne and pose the threat of an American rendezvous with the French Fourth Army to the northwest. Liggett believed that this maneuver would put the German Army in a much more precarious position and if the German forces did not react too quickly, would trap a large segment of their troops. Finally, Pershing agreed.

As the reorganization and the strategic planning were being accomplished the French government and the Allied commanders were pressuring Foch to 'do something with the Americans.' Complaints were being voiced that the Americans obviously could not take their objectives, but Foch defended Pershing's armies. He pointed out that it had only been a matter of months since the Americans had been permitted to form their separate army and that it would take them time to learn the tactical lessons which, through

Left: American soldiers wearing German body armor and helmets captured during the Meuse battle. The soldier at the right has also captured a German antitank rifle.
Far right: Brigadier General Douglas MacArthur in a characteristically photogenic pose outside his headquarters.
Below: An American tank unit advances in the final days of the war.

experience, came easily to the French and British. Foch's staunch support averted what might have become a very unpleasant incident. Any overbearing interference by the Allied commanders or governments could have produced a rift in the cooperation between the Allied and American armies that might well have resulted in defeat.

Of major importance in the last week of October were the numbers of peace feelers being sent out to the United States by Germany. The success and strength of the Allied offensive on the northern front and the dedication of the American forces had finally put a sense of desperation into the German military machine. The Allies, realizing that Germany could possibly drag the war out for yet another year, began to look seriously for a means of ending the conflict. However, the Allied command had no intention of lessening the pressure on the German armies. They wanted Germany to surrender, not bargain.

On 1 November 1918 Liggett's strategy was put into operation. On the front an American line more than 15 miles long stretched from the Argonne Forest to the Meuse. On the left flank in the Argonne were the 78th and 77th Divisions. In the center, left to right were the 80th, 2nd, and 89th Divisions. On the right flank stood the 90th then the 5th Divisions, with the 5th bordering the Meuse River. At 0330 hours an artillery bombardment of the German defenses began and at 0530 hours the divisions moved forward. The central line moved ahead with lightning speed and sent back reports to the command headquarters that the enemy could be classified as 'in full retreat.' But the far left flank was encountering the usual difficulty in passing through the Argonne. On 2 November the 78th and 77th Divisions finally pushed forward and together with the American center divisions they advanced to the village of Fosse, some seven miles into enemy territory. The German forces continued to withdraw toward Sedan. The right flank was desperately attempting to dislodge the German forces they opposed from the banks of the Meuse.

By 3 November, after a rapid march forward, sections of the 2nd Division passed north of Belval and were on their way to Beaumont. The following day the left flank divisions moved clear of the Argonne, north then east. The American line had swung in a massive pivot with the positions of the 5th Division on the Meuse at its base. The German forces had their backs to the Meuse and it was obvious that their defeat was imminent.

On 5 November Pershing, aware that the Germans were beaten, concerned himself with battle honors. Instead of continuing to spur the drive on he focussed his attention on Sedan, sending a request to the commander of the French Fourth Army, General Maistre, to ask that the American First Army be allowed to move north toward that important city. The 42nd and 77th Divisions lay closest to Sedan and would have

been the logical choice for an advance to the city. However, the 1st Division, which as the senior unit had always been a favorite with Pershing, was given the order to move toward Sedan. The weary 1st was pulled from the line and sent on a quick march north, to the rear of the 77th and Rainbow Divisions. The men were told nothing of their objectives and rumors began to circulate that a German counterattack had broken through and the 1st was being maneuvered to fill the gap. In the confusion units of the 1st Division stumbled upon the headquarters of the 42nd Division and promptly captured the division's staff. It was said that General Douglas MacArthur, commander of the 42nd, never forgave Colonel George Marshall, the First Army's operations officer, for the indignity perpetrated by one of his divisions. MacArthur added that while he could understand the confusion which created the incident he could not bear the accusation that he was a German.

The situation was one of complete chaos with troops so entangled behind their own lines that Liggett stepped in, overriding his staff and divisional commanders and ordering an immediate halt to all American movement in the direction of Sedan. He then by-passed Pershing's authority and sent a cordial message to Maistre offering the French Fourth Army the privilege of entering the city where less than 50

Above: Two French peasants greet the American soldiers who liberated them. The men are from the 77th Division seen here on 6 November at Brielles sur Bar, Ardennes.
Left: Soldiers of the 64th Regiment, 7th Division, cheer at news of the Armistice.
Right: Relaxing in the trenches with a meal and a bottle of wine.

years before the Germans had dealt the French a bitter defeat. If it had not been that the German forces were for all purposes beaten, the irresponsible Sedan affair could have been disastrous. In a full inquiry into the incident Pershing stated that as the war was almost over and no real harm had been done there was no point in pursuing the investigation. Perhaps he hoped that his role would be quickly forgotten.

By 7 and 8 November negotiations between the belligerent nations were under way in earnest. The German Army had given its support to the formation of a new government, handing Kaiser Wilhelm the bitter blow that he was no longer ruler of Germany. When he challenged the new republic's right to force his abdication the Chief of Staff Paul von Hindenburg informed him that if the need arose the German Army would stop him from attempting to regain control of the country. On 9 November Kaiser Wilhelm boarded a train for Holland where he would remain for the rest of his life.

On the eleventh hour of the eleventh day of the eleventh month of 1918 the armistice came into force and the war was ended. On all fronts the men could not believe that it was finally over and peculiar forms of insanity spread through the armies. As the hour of the armistice approached the men of the opposing armies fired their rifles and machine guns, not to kill but apparently to see who would be the last to fire a shot in the war. Artillery fired at an incredible rate as if wanting to have no ammunition left when the peace was made. Many incidents were recorded of each member of artillery brigades, from commander to clerk walking forward to fire the guns one last time. One battery ran string from a gun to each man of its 200-strong unit so that they could all fire the last round simultaneously. Not all the apparent lunacy was frivolous. Along the lines Allied and German soldiers, for reasons known only to themselves, chose the final minutes of war as the appointed hour of their death. It was an eerie time. One example was Private Henry Gunther of the 79th Division, known as the last American to be killed by the enemy. As the armistice was about to come into force he charged a German machine-gun position claiming that in so doing he could regain the rank of sergeant from which he had been demoted. The American soldiers tried to call him back and the German gunners waved him away as neither side wanted to see any more senseless bloodshed. When it became obvious to the German soldiers that Gunther was bent on killing them and was in fact almost on top of their position, they fired.

Suddenly the firing ceased and what was called a 'terrible silence' moved over the entire front. Men lay in their trenches unable to believe that endless fighting had in fact come to an end. Those who were there said that a cheer then began to spread along the Allied and German lines like a wave. Men screamed and cried and some just lay down in their trenches and went immediately into a sound sleep. The 'Great War' was over.

6 PEACE AND DISILLUSION

Although the fighting stopped that eleventh day of November the peace that was made gave a far less certain view of the future than the armistice predicted. Germany had made a desperate bid to win the war before the American involvement could have a serious impact. Failing that Germany had chosen to take a primarily defensive stance, protecting the areas that had already been taken. As long as German soil was not violated the Kaiser was willing to resist and the old enemies, Germany, England and France with their respective allies could continue to fight the war

indefinitely. But America had another effect toward bringing peace aside from the troops, materiel and supplies sent to Europe. On 8 January 1918 President Wilson had made a speech before Congress which diverged from the usual rhetoric of 'driving on,' 'crushing the enemy' and who the guilty and innocent parties of the war were. His speech was aimed at the possibilities of world peace as a result of the war that was raging. The principal aspects of the speech would become known as Wilson's Fourteen Points.

Through the use of his Fourteen Point program

Wilson believed that the war could be brought to an end with the dignity of the involved parties kept intact. It was also part of his plan to restore Europe to its pre-war status quo. At the time the speech was given Germany was not interested and was involved in the Treaty of Brest-Litovsk which concentrated on the dismembering of Russia and the prospect of a final offensive in the west using troops released from the Russian Front. However, as the months wore on and the last German offensive failed the concept behind Wilson's plan became increasingly acceptable to the German command. When Germany finally agreed to and signed the armistice it was with the understanding that a peace would be reached with the Fourteen Points as the basis for the final treaty. In essence the Fourteen Points for world peace were:

1. The abolition of secret treaties between governments.
2. The preservation of the neutrality and freedom of the seas.
3. The elimination of economic barriers between nations.
4. Armament reductions.
5. Consideration for the rights of colonial subjects.
6. Halt to foreign interference in Russian affairs.
7. Foreign evacuation and restoration of Belgium.
8. Return of Alsace and Lorraine to France.
9. Reevaluation of Italy's borders in accordance with nationality.
10. Autonomy for the peoples of Austria-Hungary.
11. Foreign evacuation of Rumania, Serbia and Montenegro with Serbia given access to the sea.
12. The Ottoman Empire to give rights of autonomous development to non-Turkish peoples and access to the Dardenelles for shipping of all nations.
13. Establishment of an independent Poland with sea access.
14. Formation of a general assembly of all nations to preserve world peace.

Around the world the points were given token acclaim. In the aftermath of their revolution the Soviets found the points acceptable and in keeping with the Communist party line. Italy, as well as Austria-Hungary and Germany, agreed that on the principles of the points a peace could be negotiated. However there were men of power world wide who viewed Wilson's proposals as 'idealistic hogwash' and as a clear indication that the American President had a naive view of the European situation.

Wilson's concepts, however idealistic, were founded on an attempt to remove several primary sources of

Above: The Moselle River and the town and castle of Cocheur, HQ of IV Corps of the US Army of Occupation, Germany 1919.
Left: Armistice celebrations Battery D, 105th Field Artillery.
Below: Soldiers of 1st Division by the Rhine, December 1918.

61

Above: Some of the American leaders arrive home in New York.
At right, General Pershing, the Commander in Chief, and second left,
Colonel Marshall, who became Chief of Staff of the US Army in
World War II.
Right: A crowded troopship arrives in Hoboken, New Jersey.

irritation among nations. The persistent intertwining of secret treaties and agreements created a cycle of negotiations by nations who felt compelled to plot because they were never sure what was going on behind closed doors with their friends and enemies. The neutrality of the seas, the removal of economic blockades and the reduction of arms were fundamental issues in the pursuit of a lasting peace. Wilson made particular reference to the claims and rights of colonial peoples, as well as those areas which had traditionally been juggled to and fro such as Alsace and Lorraine. These problems were also one of the major roots of war. He proposed referenda which would give people in such areas the right to choose independence from or adherence to a particular country.

When it was apparent that the war was lost Germany had no problem accepting Wilson's primary points. The German colonies had already been lost during the war so there was no argument there. The idea of former borders being reestablished saddened the German command but would not be intolerable. The Polish issue had been raised in diplomatic circles for years and Wilson saw this as the perfect time to act in the debate. Unfortunately Wilson would go to the peace conferences with the same idealistic view portrayed in his Fourteen Points and Germany would go expecting 'justice.' France and Britain would go in the full knowledge that they would get what they wanted.

It is impossible to view the end of World War I without seeing the seeds of World War II being sown. It is certainly obvious in retrospect, but even at the time the evidence was unmistakable to some. In the words of General Tasker H Bliss after the negotiations, 'We are in for a high period, to be followed by a low period. Then there will be the Devil to pay all around the world.' However, the world leaders went merrily on their course. Although the armistice had been signed and Germany would look to Wilson's points as the foundation of the treaty, 1919 would bring a final treaty that would go to extremes away from the non-vindictive terms that were first proposed.

Wilson's ideals were fine, but he was no match for such staunch diplomats as Britain's Lloyd George and the old French 'Tiger' Clemenceau. Wilson's dream of an organization of nations, to be known as the League of Nations, would overshadow his judgment and cause him to grant concessions to Lloyd George and Clemenceau in the hope that they would support his League. In so doing he permitted them to change the framework of the peace negotiations. Britain and France would take what they wanted and would force Germany to accept full guilt for the war. It would be a

repetition of the long history of European wars with the vanquished subjugated and the victors taking their hollow revenge. Germany would be divided, occupied and saddled with reparation debts. Wilson signed the Treaty of Versailles in search of his League of Nations, but he had given up a great deal for nothing. The American Congress refused to ratify the treaty and the United States refused to enter the League. The war did not result in world peace, disarmament or democracy.

However, from a military viewpoint World War I had offered a profitable hard knocks education. In the relatively short time that America participated in the war it demonstrated that it had the capacity for correlating the four basic ingredients, manpower, manufacturing, transportation and focussed dedication, necessary to fight a modern war on an equal footing with the acknowledged world powers. Against the odds the young nation proved that its very youth gave

it the capacity for rapid adaptation to the need presented. The lessons learned on the mobilization of America in the areas of manpower, industry, agriculture, and common spirit were valuable but would be lost sight of in the chaos of the post war era.

The war in Europe had claimed approximately 26,000,000 lives, half of them combatants and the other half civilians. Of that number 116,516 were American with another 210,000 wounded. When the survivors returned they faced a depressed economy, strikes, racial tensions, riots and a fading hope that the world would ever recover. Even the simple issue of the soldier's bonus was forgotten by the government they had served. The United States, although now considered one of the three major world powers, would return to a period of isolationism, disillusioned once again with the ways of Europe. In the cold light of reality the great adventure amounted to little more than a great disenchantment.

INDEX

Acknowledgments

The author would like to thank Adrian Hodgkins who designed this book, Richard Natkiel who drew the maps and Penny Murphy who compiled the index. The agencies listed below kindly provided the illustrations.

Bundesarchiv (via R Hunt): 8–9
Robert Hunt: 6, 7 left, 8 lower, 9, 11 right, 15 top, 19, 26–27 top, 35 top
Imperial War Museum (via R Hunt): 12 top, 17 center, 20, 22, 24–25, 29, 42–43, 47 left
National Archives (US): 12 center & lower, 13, 14 lower, 16, 17 top & bottom, 18 bottom, 21, 23, 26 top, 28, 32, 33, 38 left, 40–41 all three, 43 bottom, 44, 45, 46, 46–47 both, 49 both, 54 top, 55, 56 both, 57, 58 both, 60, 61 both
National Archives (via R Hunt): 18 top & center, 24, 32 top, 34, 35 bottom, 36–37 all three, 51, 52–53, 54 bottom, 62, 63
Smithsonian Institute: 22–23, 31
US Air Force: 39 all three, 43 top
US Army: 11 left, 59 (via R Hunt)
US Marines: 14 top
US Navy: 7 right, 15 lower.